Quakers in India: A Forgotten Century

Quakers in India

A Forgotten Century

MARJORIE SYKES

London
GEORGE ALLEN & UNWIN
Boston   Sydney

GEORGE ALLEN & UNWIN LTD
40 Museum Street, London WC1A 1LU

© George Allen & Unwin (Publishers) Ltd, 1980

British Library Cataloguing in Publication Data

Sykes, Marjorie
  Quakers in India.
  1. Friends in India
  I. Title
  289.6′54   BX7716.I5   80–40223

  ISBN 0–04–275003–2

Set in 10 on 12 point Times by Inforum Limited, Portsmouth
and printed in Great Britain
by Biddles Ltd, Guildford, Surrey

Foreword

William Martin Wood, one of the Quakers whose work in India is described in this book, used to quote what he said was an Egyptian proverb: 'The mother of foresight looks backwards'. And, although human beings are reputed to be slow to learn foresight from history, there may be some interest in looking backwards at the earlier stages of the Quaker intercourse with India as it developed in the century preceding Indian independence.

The first suggestion that such a book might be useful came from Indian friends who had known Quakers in India during the last two decades and were curious about how the various Quaker centres and projects had come into existence. The two books previously written do not meet the need and are both out of print. Henry T Hodgkin's *Friends Beyond Seas* (1916) contains some chapters about India, but is limited to the missionary work undertaken by British Friends during the preceding fifty years. Horace Alexander's pamphlet *Quakerism and India* (1945) is a first-hand but inevitably brief account of the work of the Friends Ambulance Unit in India during the Second World War, set against the background of larger issues which the title suggests, and opened up a number of lines of inquiry which it seemed useful to pursue.

The studies which follow trace the development of Quaker interest in India from 1815 onwards. That interest followed a characteristic Quaker pattern in that it arose out of the deeply felt concern of individuals whose enthusiasm won the support of others. But the individual concerns themselves were generated by a complex interplay of circumstance in which both the general climate of thought and opinion and the influence of individuals outside the Society of Friends played a large part. Neither in India nor anywhere else did Quakers think and act in isolation; these studies, small as they are, are part of a larger story than that of the Society of Friends. 'Such is the unity of all history', wrote F. W. Maitland, 'that anyone who attempts to tell a piece of it must feel that his first sentence tears a seamless web.' The Quaker interests on which we focus take much of their meaning from the tapestry of history of which they are a part.

The book concentrates on the contributions made by individuals rather than on the activities carried on in Quaker projects and institutions. Many of the things which bulk most largely in the archives of the Quaker Service Committees in England and the United States, Canada and Australia, find little or no place in its pages. There are a number of reasons for this choice. One is in the very existence of those bulky archives themselves. The records are *there*, and along with the more impersonal reports they contain much vivid and valuable material about individual Quakers who have worked in India during the last thirty or forty years. The present writer is too close to these projects, and has been too much involved with some of them, to feel able to evaluate them adequately. The omission of any discussion of them does *not* mean that they are considered unimportant. Still less does the omission of any tribute to scores of Quakers who have worked in them, and who are remembered in India with affection and respect, mean that their contributions are ignored or unappreciated. It simply means that this is not that kind of book.

On the other hand there have been a considerable number of Quaker friends of India, particularly in the long pre-independence period, of whom the official Quaker archives have no record at all, because they did not go to India as representatives of any corporate Quaker body. They lived in India as individuals or families, following their own profession and earning an independent livelihood as they would have done in England. Their contribution to mutual understanding between Quakers and kindred spirits in India, and between India and the West, is not easy to define, but it is none the less real. Circumstances brought me into touch with some of them, in the 1920s and 1930s, and my own familiarity with India over many years has enabled me to trace material concerning them which might otherwise have been lost.

It has been less easy to piece together the contributions made by the nineteenth-century Quakers, though here too some familiarity with the Indian background has helped in interpreting the fragmentary records that remain. The pursuit of these records, from one small clue to the next, has sometimes had all the zest of a detective story, and sometimes all the satisfaction of watching bits of a jigsaw puzzle, one after another, drop into place. What emerges, I hope, is a series of sketches of real people in all their varied individuality. The sketches are incomplete, and most of the people have been forgotten, but the questions of principle and policy with which they struggled are still, in their essence, alive today.

Whatever success has attended this detective work is due to the generosity and patience of almost innumerable people, from the staff of the Friends House Library in London and of the Swarthmore and Haverford College libraries in the United States to the many personal friends in India, Britain and elsewhere who have helped to unearth tiny but often significant scraps of evidence from all kinds of unexpected places. Such friends are too numerous to name; those who read this will know that I remember them with gratitude, as also those who helped to type successive drafts. I wish also to record my appreciation of the staffs of public libraries, and the keepers of official records and archives of many kinds, who have answered letters and personal inquiries with an unvarying courtesy and thoroughness to which this book owes much.

One of the minor problems of such a study as this is the changing meaning and the changing emotional flavour of some of the words used. One such word is 'native'. In the period covered by the earlier chapters of this book it carried its literal meaning; two British friends of the British India Society were quite correctly described as 'natives' of India – they were born there. It was not until the end of the nineteenth century that one of Martin Wood's journalist friends felt constrained to avoid the word because of its contemptuous overtones. 'Anglo-Indian' during the same period meant an English person resident in India; communities of mixed racial origin were known as 'East Indian'. Before the Mutiny 'empire' meant an *equal* partnership of peoples; 'imperialist' overtones are a more recent growth. The change in the connotation of 'Hindu' is more subtle. It is a Persian adjective meaning 'Indian', and down to the end of the nineteenth century it was used to denote the distinctive culture of the Indian subcontinent. This included religious practice but was not limited to it. A consciousness of difference between Muslim and Hindu often included that of a different land of origin – many noble

Muslim families had Persian or Afghan roots. When people referred to Hindu Christians or Hindu Quakers they were talking of
cultural affinities, not of religious belief. The limitation of the term
to religion began during the closing years of the nineteenth century,
but the older use continued for some time.

Finally I have 'tried to understand', in the spirit described by
Peter Geyl in *The Use and Abuse of History*. If I have succeeded in
some measure, 'looking backwards' will not have been in vain:

> The most we can ever hope for is a partial rendering, an approx-
> imation, of the real truth about the past. [But] even a partial
> conquest of reality may help to divert a student's mind from
> one-sided admiration or detraction; the mind will become aware
> of finer shadings where before there was only the crude contrast
> between black and white. . . . The true historian will neither
> sneer nor curse, he will try to understand.

MARJORIE SYKES

Contents

I

Prologue 1659

The lamps are different but the light is the same; it comes from Beyond.

Jalaluddin Rumi

A century ago the word 'Quaker' was looked on with disfavour among members of the Religious Society of Friends. The editor of their *Monthly Record* in London declared in 1869 that 'the unmeaning and reproachful term *Quaker* is banished from our pages and will not be inserted again'. Today, in India, Pakistan and Bangladesh, the word is neither unmeaning nor reproachful. During the last fifty years Quakers have become widely known, and have been regarded, in a very real sense, as *friends*.

During the twenty years preceding the independence and partition of the subcontinent, when 'India' was one political unit, those who led her freedom struggle came to know Quakers in Britain as people who were ready to *listen*, to try to understand, and to act as interpreters and intermediaries between them and the British Government. These Quakers did not stand aloof, as some British officials of the 1920s seemed to do; they paid personal visits to India, they studied her aspirations on the spot, they lived alongside her leaders and talked with them intimately and at leisure. By the time Mahatma Gandhi visited London for the Round Table Conference of 1931 he had several trusted Quaker friends; before he left London he had many more. The next fifteen years of strenuous political confrontations and negotiations saw Quakers taking a leading part in the honourable settlement of differences through the India Conciliation Group. Horace Alexander and Agatha Harrison in particular became familiar figures in India; many doors were open to them.

The same years saw the growth of a Quaker concern to share in the work of social renewal and education which Gandhi called his 'constructive programme'. In the Friends Rural Centre at Rasulia in central India imaginative plans for awakening and developing the human potential of the village people were carried out under Quaker leadership by men and women of many races and faiths. It was the confidence inspired by such Quakers and others like them, and in particular by Horace Alexander's steady integrity, that made it possible for the Friends Ambulance Unit to work in 1942–3 in politically sensitive disaster areas like Bengal and Orissa, with the co-operation both of British officials and of Indian nationalists. In 1947 the same confidence in Quaker integrity enabled Quaker service teams to work with the governments of newly independent India and Pakistan for the uprooted populations on both sides of the new frontiers. Scores of young Quakers from many countries took part in such projects; the friendships they made and the insights they gained have enriched their lives ever since.

This vigorous Quaker intercourse with the Indian subcontinent did not develop suddenly out of nothing in the years around 1930. A number of factors had been at work to pave the way. One of the most potent influences was that of C. F. Andrews, who by 1930 had been in touch with some young Quakers for nearly twenty years, and had shared with them his unrivalled knowledge of nationalist India and his enthusiasm for the thought and work of his two great Indian friends, Rabindranath Tagore and Mohandas Karamchand Gandhi. Quaker university students in the first decade of the century had been touched by the renaissance of Quaker religious life which had begun in the previous generation; many of them were rediscovering, with excitement and enthusiasm, the liberating power of the original Quaker faith. After the First World War Quakers were seeking with a new urgency the foundations of a just social order and of a peaceful world, and they were strongly attracted to Tagore and Gandhi by the many affinities between their own ethical and religious principles and those of the Indian thinkers. It was natural that they should respond to Tagore's emphasis on the spiritual dimensions of India's life, and to Gandhi's declaration that there could be no real national freedom without justice and human dignity for the outcaste and despised. Gandhi's method of *satyagraha*, of fearless, open, non-violent disobedience to laws believed to be wrong, vividly recalled the peaceful, open disobedience of seventeenth-century Quakers in Britain to laws which their consciences could not accept.

Satyagraha was not a mere matter of expediency; it expressed a faith in the ultimate power of Truth. Gandhi's faith, like Tagore's, had been nurtured by movements of the human spirit in India which in some ways were strikingly parallel to those movements of the human spirit in Europe out of which Quakerism sprang. In both was the conviction that Truth must irradiate all the business of daily living, and bring justice and mercy, righteousness and peace, into the common intercourse of humanity.

The story of the beginning of Quakerism has often been told. The movement took shape in England between the years 1647 and 1652, amid the upheavals of civil war and of Cromwell's Commonwealth. The churches were torn by sectarian strife, and many turned from them in despair, finding no food for their souls. 'The hungry sheep look up and are not fed,' wrote the poet Milton in indignation and compassion. It was among such seeking souls that the young George Fox, who had himself been through the darkness of despair, created the joyful, fearless fellowship which came to call itself the Religious Society of Friends, and which its enemies in mockery called 'Quaker'.

George Fox appealed to a new kind of authority, not the outward authority of church or scripture, but the inward authority of experience. In this he showed himself a man of his time. During the same years in which he was declaring the 'Truth' which he knew 'experimentally' some of his most brilliant contemporaries were meeting (in what was to become the Royal Society) to explore by observation and experiment the processes of the natural world. Both in science and in religion long-unquestioned authority was being challenged by an appeal to human reason and human experience.

George Fox's inward assurance was rooted in a mystical experience in which he had known Christ Jesus as a living presence, an 'Inward Teacher'. For him it was a revolutionary personal discovery, and it sent him out to proclaim 'Christ the new and living way . . . the spirit of Truth in the inward parts'. In fact, there were others who taught in the same spirit. The saintly Benjamin Whichcote of Cambridge declared the essence of religion to be that Christ should be 'inwardly felt as a principle of divine life within us', and his test like Fox's was experimental and practical. 'Give me a religion,' he wrote, 'which doth attain *real* effects' – a purified life, a growth in holiness. Unless these effects are there, he said, the doctrine that Christ has 'washed away our sins in his blood' is 'a mere dream or opinion'.

Whichcote was one of the small group of thinkers known as the Cambridge Platonists, who saw clearly that the appeal to experience meant a new view not only of doctrine but of human nature itself. In contrast to the commonly held ideas of the 'total depravity' of 'fallen' mankind, they loved to quote the Biblical saying that 'the spirit of man is a candle of the Lord'.[1] The divine light in the candle might be enfeebled and obscured by human fear and sin, but it was there, able to illuminate reason and conscience and to guide judgement. Fox shared their faith. 'The Lord opened to me by his invisible power', he wrote, 'how that everyone was enlightened by the divine light of Christ, and I saw it shine through all.'

This faith in the power of the human spirit to grow in the knowledge of right and wrong led Quakers and others to question also the idea of the final authority of the Bible. 'The Spirit which is given us is a more certain guide than Scripture,' said Milton, and a Quaker scholar, Samuel Fisher, drew attention to the doubt cast on parts of the text by ambiguities of interpretation and translation. Fox, who knew and loved the treasures of the Bible, nevertheless called it 'a declaration of the fountain, not the fountain itself'. The essential thing was to know for oneself the spirit which had inspired the Scripture: 'What canst *thou* say? What *thou* speakest, is it inwardly from God?'

From this it followed that the Quakers stood strongly with Whichcote and with Milton for freedom of conscience and freedom of speech. 'Let Truth and Falsehood grapple!' wrote Milton in his magnificent defence of freedom of printing. 'Who ever knew Truth worsted in a fair and open encounter?' Early Quaker history records the costly struggles to win these freedoms, both for themselves and for others.

Fox and his first followers carried this revolutionary religious message into the farms and market-places of every corner of England. They were warmly welcomed, they were also violently opposed. They stood up in the churches (which Fox called 'steeplehouses') and challenged the authority of their 'hireling' priests. They were often beaten and abused, but the Truth was not worsted, and many joined them. The Quaker fellowship swallowed up social distinctions, for because the Light 'shone through all' every human being was worthy of respect. Aristocrat and working farmer, scholar and rough sailor, mistress and maidservant, 'were knit to the Lord and one another in true and fervent love'.[2] They came together in silence to seek the 'Inward Teacher'; those present were 'like living coals warming one another', and the sense of a holy Presence would often set them all 'quaking'. At such times anyone present, man or woman, learned or unlettered, might be impelled to speak words which had power to help them all. The nickname 'Quaker' came to be accepted as an honourable name.

Their experience of spiritual equality made Quakers sensitive to social injustice and made them champions of the oppressed. At that time great economic changes were taking place, and there was much suffering among the powerless poor. Quakers spoke out about the 'horrible injustice' of the exploitation which provided luxuries for the few. Their own plain and simple ways of dress and living were a protest against the extravagances of the fashions of the time. Poverty, declared the Quaker James Nayler, was *not* the will of God, but the work of 'covetous cruel oppressors'.[3] 'Oh England, my native country, come to judgement,' cried William Penn. 'Bring thy deeds to the Light; see whether they are wrought in God or no.' William Penn worked out the principles of justice and humanity in his 'holy experiment' in civil government in Pennsylvania; the Quakers dealt with American Indians and with African slaves as human beings worthy of respect. In England they suffered a good deal because they refused to observe the customary courtesies of speech and manners by which some human beings were honoured more than others.[4] They also refused to take an oath, saying that Yes should be Yes, and No should be No, on *all* occasions.

Quakers described their struggle against 'corruptions and lusts' as 'the Lamb's war'. They were convinced, however, that the spirit of Christ would never allow them to use outward weapons either in this 'war' or in any other. 'Patience must get the victory', wrote George Fox, 'and answer to that of God in every one and will bring every one from the contrary.'[5] If we reflect that in Fox's time the word 'patience' was nearer than it is now to its original meaning of 'endurance of suffering', we shall see how that advice anticipates Gandhi's faith in the ultimate triumph of *satyagraha*.

The Quakers believed that their message was for all humanity, not merely for England or for Christians. Within a few years many of them were making long and dangerous journeys in order to direct all they could reach to 'that grace and spirit of God in them which they have from God in their hearts'. Seventeenth-century England, whose ships traded round the world, was vividly aware of the other world religions, of 'heathens, Turks and Jews' as the phrase went, and the Quaker travellers would expect to find much outward variety of religious practice. It did not trouble them. 'Though the way seems to thee divers,' wrote Fox, 'yet judge not the way lest thou judge the Lord; several ways hath God to bring his people out by.'[6] The Cambridge Platonists shared this universal outlook, and many of them would have echoed Penn's famous words: 'The humble, meek, merciful, just, pious and devout souls are everywhere of one religion, . . . though the divers liveries they wear here makes them strangers.'[7]

India was one of the countries which Quakers tried to reach. Several attempts failed, but it is *possible* that one succeeded. In August 1661 George Fox sent out a newsletter in which he mentioned a Friend who was then visiting him. The Friend, he wrote, 'hath been three years *out in the East Indies*; [he] hath done much service and brings a good report of many that received his testimony; [he] hath travelled to many nations and islands.'[8] That is all; the Friend is not named, nor any of the 'many nations' which he visited. At the time, a visit to India might have been comparatively easy. During the Civil War and the Commonwealth the East India Company had been too crippled by exactions from both sides to be able to enforce its trade monopoly, and many private adventurers took the chance of doing some profitable business. One such ship, in 1658 or 1659, *might* have carried a Quaker passenger.

If such a traveller did reach India, it was not wonderful that he should have found 'many that received his testimony'. As has been said, there were movements of the spirit in seventeenth-century India with which Quakers would have felt themselves in sympathy. Some knowledge of these will be helpful in understanding the background of the historical contacts of later centuries.

All over India the way of *bhakti-yoga*, loving personal devotion, was recognised as a valid spiritual path alongside *jnana-yoga*, the way of impersonal knowledge. Like the inward experience of Quakerism, it overflowed in fellowship and compassion, and broke through the social barriers of class and caste, of sect and sex. Many of its saints were women, both princesses and paupers. Devotees travelled the roads of India much as Quaker 'publishers of Truth' travelled the roads of England; in 1659 a Quaker inquirer could not have failed to meet them.

Many of the songs and legends of the *bhaktas* were already centuries old, especially in the south. They taught that the visible temple was no more than a symbol of an inward and universal

Reality. One legend tells how Avvaiyar, the Wise Woman, being wearied by travel, stretched her tired old limbs under a tree by the roadside and slept. Presently she was rudely awakened; angry villagers were abusing her for insulting their god by lying with her feet pointed towards his shrine. 'My friends,' she said gently, 'is there any place where God is *not* present? Show me, and there I will point my feet.'

Avvaiyar's fellow countryman Appar is said to have served the villages through which he passed by cleaning the moss and weeds from their little shrines. But he himself worshipped inwardly, 'in spirit and in truth':

> Our body is the shrine, the steadfast mind is the worshipper.
> We have cleansed the shrine with truth, and within it
> we have enthroned the Lord, the jewel of our minds.
> As others offer their dainties, made of *ghee* and milk,
> so we lay at his feet our gift of love.

Appar knew an Inward Light, 'the jewelled lamp that shines in the heart', 'the Teacher that enters the soul'. Centuries later the Bauls of Bengal, disciples of the saint Chaitanya, were also worshipping 'the Man of the Heart', and some of them were rejecting the outward forms of religion in language as blunt as Fox's condemnations of 'steeple-houses' and 'hireling priests':

> Thy path, O Lord, is hidden by mosque and temple.
> Thy voice I hear, but priest and guru bar the way.

In general, however, there is little condemnation, and much emphasis on the qualities of spirit that make for unity and righteousness. A Quaker would have recognised the 'one religion' of which Penn had written in the 'eight flowers dear to the Lord' which are listed in the *Vishnu Purana*: harmlessness and self-mastery, loving-kindness and forgiveness, peace and endurance, piety and truth. Muslim devotees recognised them too. 'Though the Hindu's religious practice is not mine,' wrote Amir Khusro, 'yet are there many truths which he and I hold in common.'[9] One of the greatest of the *bhaktas*, the poet-weaver Kabir, was himself of Muslim origin; a constantly recurring theme in his poems is the power of real religious experience to transcend the divisions of caste and creed. 'Heaven is in the company of the saint,' he declared – and what a mixed company it was!

> It is but folly to ask what the caste of a saint may be.
> The barber has sought God, the washerman and the carpenter ...
> Hindu and Muslim alike have reached that goal
> where remains no mark of distinction.

Another of Kabir's poems is a call to what Quakers called 'the Lamb's war':

> In the field of the body a great war goes forward
>   against passion, anger, pride and greed.
> The battle is joined, for purity and truth;
>   the sword of His Name rings aloud.

The theme of the Lamb's war appears too in one of the best known and best loved stories in India, the *Ramayana*. When the unarmed hero Rama is told that Ravana, king of unrighteousness, is coming in his war-chariot to do battle, he replies:

> The chariot which will bring victory is of another kind. Courage and fortitude are its wheels, truthfulness and upright conduct its banner and its standard. The horses are self-control and good-will, harnessed with cords of forgiveness and compassion.

There, in Indian imagery, is Fox's teaching about the patience which must get the victory.

These songs and stories had been handed down from an earlier age, but in 1659 there were in India two living saints whose work was later to have a special interest for Quakers. One of them was a Muslim saint or *pir*, who had been born in 1597 in the Meo Muslim community of north-west India. It is said that his name was Lal Das, and that the Mogul prince Dara Shikoh had a great respect for him. He gathered together a brotherhood known as the Sauds, who like Kabir earned their bread by their own labour, drew Hindus and Muslims together, and built mosques and temples side by side. They lived and worshipped in a great simplicity; like Quakers they refused to take an oath. The brotherhood was open to all, and in later years attracted many Hindus, who in accordance with their own tradition referred to the *pir* as their *sat-guru*, teacher of Truth.[10]

The other saint was the Marathi poet Tukaram, who was also George Fox's contemporary. He was of 'low' caste, a Sudra, perhaps a grain-seller, and it is said that he was persecuted by Brahmins who resented the popularity of his religious teaching. The teaching was given in songs, in the imagery of familiar village life, and it is said that the birds would come and perch on his shoulders as he sang them in the temple courtyard. A few quotations will show why his spirit is so congenial to Quakers:

> Even an earthenware pot is honoured,
> it is set on the head, and carried high,
> because in it is the life-giving water.
> *Show reverence to humanity, because of God within humanity.*
>
> Rough wooden casks are honoured,
> the merchant receives them gladly,
> because in them is the precious grain.
> *Show reverence to humanity, because of God within humanity.*

Like Fox, he spoke with the authority of inward experience:

> When a child is learning to write, pebbles are placed to guide him.
> But when he knows the letters' shapes, what need has he of pebbles?
> And I, my friends, I know, I *know*.

For him, as for Quakers, religion must bear fruit in action:

> If a man is to show forth thy praise, his deeds must speak more loudly than words.
> He is a true saint who befriends the weary and the persecuted,
> and where he is the Lord himself is found.[11]

These quotations might be almost infinitely multiplied. They afford a glimpse of some of the sources from which not only Tagore and Gandhi, but many more of the Indians who worked most closely with Quakers, drew insight and inward strength. If any Quaker did visit India about 1659, what an encounter there might have been! But that is pure conjecture; nearly two hundred years were to pass before any actual contact is recorded, and by that time great changes had taken place both in India and in the Society of Friends.

II

Two Centuries of Change 1659—1859

There were very tender consciences in the borderland where
Quakerism and Evangelicalism met.

Edmund Knox, Bishop of Manchester

The year 1659 may be regarded as a turning-point in Indian history.
For a century past, the wealth and splendour of India had been the
wonder of Europe. The Mogul emperor Akbar, 'the Great', contemporary of Queen Elizabeth I of England, had ruled a prosperous
country. His empire was in practice a secular state whose
heterogeneous elements were held together by the ties of personal
loyalty which bound the great local lineages, Muslim and Rajput
alike, to the emperor; his cadres of civil and military officers were
chosen regardless of religious affiliation from the aristocratic
families who shared the Persian culture of the court.

From 1659 onwards, during the reign of the emperor Aurangzeb,
this Mogul–Persian culture was challenged by Marathas and Sikhs
on the one hand and by orthodox Muslims on the other. Aurangzeb
fought a long series of costly wars, and when he died in 1707 his
weakened empire began to fall apart. Regional governors set themselves up as independent princes; Persians, then Afghans, became
temporarily masters of Delhi, while Maratha armies terrorised the
countryside. The great irrigation works on which so much of the
well-being of India depended began to fall into decay.

The foreign trading companies established around the coasts
during Akbar's time no longer felt secure. They fortified their posts
and claimed a kind of buffer-zone of territory round about them,*
and they began to share in the general scramble for power. The
British succeeded, though not easily, in outdoing their French com-

* One method of demarcating a 'buffer-zone' will interest those who know of
Quaker 'walking purchases' in Pennsylvania. In 1690 the Marathas sold to the
English a site for a trading station at Cuddalore, together with all the land 'within the

petitors and in bringing more and more land under their own control. Many of them were mere freebooters, rapacious and ruthless, whose sole object was to return to England with a fortune in the shortest possible time. As an Indian observer wrote about 1760, 'the people under their dominion groan everywhere and are reduced to poverty and distress'.[1] In 1770 a truly appalling famine took place in Bengal, and in 1773 the Directors of the East India Company admitted what they were powerless to prevent, that 'vast fortunes have been obtained by the most tyrannic and oppressive conduct ever known'. From India, one honest man pointed out that the personal emoluments of Company servants had 'drawn Ruin upon the Country from whence such enormous stipends have so long been Drained and so shamefully applyed'.[2] The writer's words 'drained' and 'shameful' were to be echoed by many other witnesses during the next fifty years.

One might have expected that the Quakers, who had spoken out so strongly in the 1650s against the oppression of the poor in England, would have spoken out against these abuses also. William Penn, who in 1681 had initiated the Quaker 'holy experiment' in just government in Pennsylvania, had pointed out that 'Governments, like clocks, go from the motion men given them', and that 'true godliness don't turn men out of the world, but enables them to live better in it, and excites their endeavours to mend it'. By 1770, however, Quakers took a very different view: they were *not*, wrote one of them, 'the proper instrument for setting right things which may appear out of order', and they should be very cautious how they 'intermeddle in politics or government'.[3] This was not just an individual opinion; in 1780 Quakers were advised by their leaders to be on their guard against taking part in 'the petitions and protests now carrying on in various places for different puposes';[4] they were encouraged to maintain an almost monastic isolation from the political interests of their times.

The explanation of this complete change of attitude is found in Quaker history. After 1660 when Charles II was restored to the English throne all citizens were required by law to conform to the national church and swear an oath of loyalty to the national state. Quakers declared that they would gladly obey 'all just and good

---

random shot of a piece of ordnance'. The English sent to Madras for their best gun and most expert gunner! The villages thus acquired are still called the *cannonball villages*.

(Michael Edwardes, *British India*, p. 18.)

laws', but refused either to swear or to give up freedom of worship. They resorted to open, non-violent civil disobedience, which meant that thousands of them suffered repeated imprisonment in the filthy jails. The struggle continued, at intervals, for twenty-five years, until at last in 1689 the repressive laws were suspended. Many Quakers were broken in health by their sufferings; many thousands more emigrated to America to find the freedom of worship denied to them at home. Nearly all the most gifted leaders had died exhausted before relief came, and when George Fox himself died in 1691 there was no one who could take his place.

What survived was less an outgoing movement than a small introverted sect. Quakers sought less to *publish* Truth than to preserve it. They were on the defensive, and held aloof from the 'world'. They clung to the forms of speech and dress and conduct which had once testified to their belief in human equality. But the forms had lost their meaning as times and manners changed; Quakers were sometimes ridiculed for their peculiar clothes in a way that children found hard to bear.[5] Many young people rebelled against the forms; many more rebelled against the rigid marriage rules. Up to 1859 it was impossible to remain a Quaker if one married outside the Society. Hundreds of fine men and women were lost to it and very few came in; numbers steadily declined, and about 1860 reached their lowest ebb.

Another aspect of the change was that many Quakers lost the joyful confidence that 'the spirit of man is a candle of the Lord'. They came to the weekly worship with no expectation or desire that the 'Inward Teacher' would give them any message to share with others, and when meetings were held in complete silence week after week the silence itself could easily become a lifeless form. But in spite of all these weaknesses the Society did not die out. There were some sensitive men and women who did speak of the things of the spirit with humility and power. There was a loving and often lively family circle which kept the children's loyalty in spite of their impatience with the rules. Quakers possessed a quiet strength and integrity of character which earned them wide respect.

As the eighteenth century progressed many able Quakers, excluded as they then were from the universities and the learned professions, built up what have been called 'the Quaker empires' in industry, commerce and banking. They were among the pioneers of the industrial revolution which during the next two generations changed the face of England. By no means all Quakers were rich; in the middle of the nineteenth century many of them were humble, working-class people, but it was the network of wealthy, inter-related families who controlled in large measure the affairs of the Society, for it was they who had the money and the leisure to attend the Yearly Meeting, the annual gathering of British Friends in London. These families were part and parcel of the prosperous British middle class, and many of them, abandoning to a greater or less degree the Quaker social seclusion, began mixing with others and participating in their interests.

Many Quakers, along with others, felt the power of the great religious revival (the 'evangelical revival' as it came to be called[6]) which swept over Britain and America in the latter part of the eighteenth century. It brought a new warmth of devotion into the cold formalism of the churches; it broke through the complacency of the prosperous with a call to respond in the name of Christ to the desperate needs of the growing urban slums and the sufferings of the oppressed throughout the world.* It spoke of the love of God for all.

One of the fruits of this renewed religious life was the great campaign to end first the slave trade and then the institution of slavery itself. The task occupied much of the attention of British Quaker philanthropists for fifty years, from 1783 until the Emancipation Act which freed slaves in British colonies in 1833. The slave traffic across the Atlantic Ocean had been a notorious scandal for many years, and British shipping was deeply implicated, but up to the 1770s British Quakers had remained as 'quiet' about this as about the scandals of the situation in India; they had contented themselves with seeing that Quaker shipowners kept their hands clean. American Quakers in Philadelphia and New Jersey, however, kept on urging British Quakers to take more public action, and at last in 1783 London Yearly Meeting presented to Parliament a public petition against the slave trade. It was the first such petition ever to be made, and with it the Society of Friends began to 'intermeddle' once more in public affairs.

The long emancipation campaign brought Quakers into a close working partnership with men belonging to other churches who like them had been stirred by the evangelical revival. Among them were Thomas Clarkson, the 'fact-finder' of the campaign, and William Wilberforce, its Parliamentary spokesman. Wilberforce had

* The story of Elizabeth Fry's early life, conversion and subsequent prison work is especially revealing.

decided (in the spirit of William Penn) that his religious interests
ought *not* to mean withdrawal from public work: 'That would merit
no better name than desertion of the post where Providence has
placed me.'[7] His example must have encouraged his Quaker friends
to query their own Society's timid aloofness from public life.
Thomas Clarkson became so intimate with Quakers that many
people thought that he was one himself. It was during these years
that he wrote his book *A Portraiture of Quakerism*, which was
published in 1806 and widely read, and which (as we shall see)
played a part in carrying the Quaker message to India.

It was the friendships made during the emancipation campaign
which first awakened Quaker interest in India. Wilberforce himself,
and a number of those whose support he enlisted, both in Parliament and outside it, had connections with India; some of them had
held responsible official positions there. The radical humanist
Joseph Hume had spent a number of years in the service of the East
India Company before entering Parliament. Another man with
close contacts in India was Zachary Macaulay, the father of the
future Lord Macaulay. He and the Quaker William Allen worked
together to establish a colony for freed slaves in West Africa, and it
was possibly he who suggested that the Calcutta Botanical Gardens
might be able to supply suitable commercial plants for trial in the
colony. In 1811 Allen wrote to Calcutta and arranged for plant
material to be sent. The result, he recorded, 'justified my most
sanguine expectations'.[8]

Several of the former East India Company officials with whom
Quakers thus came into touch had themselves been influenced by
the evangelical revival. Among them was Wilberforce's friend
Charles Grant, who along with Wilberforce took an active part in
promoting the new foreign missionary societies which were one
fruit of the religious enthusiasm. Before Grant entered Parliament
in the 1790s he had held high official posts in India, and even while
he was there he had urged on the Governor-General, Lord Cornwallis, the need for 'missionaries to the heathen'. Cornwallis was
not enthusiastic, neither was his successor Sir John Shore. Perhaps
they were aware of the popular Indian impression of 'Christians',
vividly summed up by one observer in the words: 'Christian religion
devil religion; Christian much drunk, much do wrong, much beat,
much abuse others.'[9] 'The first duty of the English is to be better
Christians themselves,' Shore commented. Parliament agreed with
him, and in 1793 Grant and Wilberforce failed to persuade it to

modify the Company's Charter so as to permit British missionaries to enter its territory.

During the next few years, however, British fear of the 'godless' French Revolution, and the wars with France, brought about a change in the public attitude. The best defence against the threat of a similar revolution in England, it was thought, was the encouragement of religion by teaching the Bible to 'the poor'. The British and Foreign Bible Society, founded in 1804, was strongly supported by Quakers among others; Quakers themselves took the lead, a few years later, in organising the British and Foreign Schools Society, which used the Bible as its chief textbook and carried on and expanded the work begun by the Quaker teacher Joseph Lancaster among the children of the London slums. The Quakers William Allen and Stephen Grellet prepared a selection of passages, *Scripture Lessons for Schools,* for the use of the Society. In 1813 the evangelical group in Parliament succeeded in securing approval for British missionary enterprise in India, while at the same time the pressure of powerful British mercantile interests ended the Company's monopoly of Indian trade and opened Indian ports to other British shipping. The result was a tremendous increase in the numbers of British people who visited or resided in India in a private capacity, in some form of commercial, philanthropic or religious enterprise.

Unfortunately this same period saw the beginnings of a British racial arrogance which was to poison human relationships for many years. The hard-drinking 'Christian' bullies of the eighteenth century had many faults, but racial prejudice was not one of them. The change is linked to the fateful decision in the 1780s that India should be governed by an *English* system run by English officials – a decision which excluded Indians from positions of real responsibility. From then on it became usual to appoint as Governor-General a man, with no Indian experience, sent fresh from England. Lord Wellesley, appointed in 1798, was apt to treat Indians with discourtesy, and his example was followed. The overbearing rudeness of so-called 'Christian gentlemen' was added to the boorish insolence of drunken sailors and soldiers and the ruffianly tyranny of greedy indigo-planters. It is a dismal record and all too well documented.[10]

It is ironic that this should have been the background against which the missionary enthusiasts urged Britain to 'civilise and enlighten' an India which they regarded as 'sunk in darkness, vice and misery' by 'diffusing the light of the Christian religion' and introducing Western ways of life.[11] The British middle classes to which they belonged were convinced that 'the world only needed to be made like themselves';[12] Wilberforce told Parliament in 1813 that Britain could best serve India by 'the establishment of our own institutions and manners, religion and morals'. Twenty years later Lord Macaulay's work was based on the same assumptions. The missionaries who poured into India after 1814 commended Christianity to their fellow countrymen as the natural ally of British Government and British trade. A tract published in Calcutta in 1814 had as its theme 'The Advantages of Christianity in promoting the establishment and prosperity of the British Empire'; two anonymous writers of an 'Open Letter' to the Quaker shipowner James Cropper declared that 'every triumph of Christianity is the opening of a wider market for British manufactures'.[13] The missionaries worked with much selfless devotion to seek and save those whom they believed to be 'lost', but their conviction that they alone possessed the Truth and that all other religions were in error resulted (though there were noble exceptions) in an attitude of complacent ignorance and contempt towards Indian culture which strengthened the prejudices of their fellow countrymen and alienated sensitive Indians.

Yet although these Westernising trends were dominant many of the ablest men in the Company's service at that time took a very different view. They shared Warren Hastings's belief that Britain's task was to give India an *Indian* government, purged and reinvigorated, but based on Indian models and manned by Indian officials. Like Hastings, they knew India intimately and many of them identified themselves with her life.* Scholars like Sir William Jones in Bengal and Justice Erskine in Bombay helped by their researches to awaken a pride in Indian identity and Indian achievements. There were other men of outstanding quality who rejected the whole idea of Britain's 'civilising' mission. 'If there could be a trade in civilisation between India and England, it is *England* that would benefit by the import cargo,' wrote Sir Thomas Munro in 1813.[14] 'Englishmen suppose', he protested, 'that no country can be saved without English institutions. The natives of this country have enough of their own to answer every useful object of internal

---

* Jonathan Duncan, Governor of Bombay at the turn of the century, was called 'the Brahminised Englishman'. Col. Kirkpatrick of Hyderabad lived like a Mogul nobleman, spoke cultured Persian, and married a Muslim lady of good family.

administration, and we should maintain and protect them.'[15] He was thinking of institutions like the traditional village *panchayat*, whose intimate local knowledge made for wise decisions and simple speedy justice. Men like Charles Metcalfe and John Malcolm deplored any interference with these natural organs of social and political life. 'Change, to be safe and beneficial,' said John Malcolm, 'must be the work of society itself.'[16]

These same men condemned the exclusion of Indians from all responsible share in the government of their country as a *moral* injury, calculated to 'debase the whole people'; 'People may be greatly injured', reported Munro, 'by what we mean for their good';[17] the physical security which British rule had conferred* would be too dearly bought if it meant the sacrifice of independence and national self-respect. 'It is better for our honour and our interest', wrote Mountstuart Elphinstone of Bombay, 'that we should resign our power into the hands of the people for whose benefit it is entrusted to us.'[18] The Governor-General, Lord Hastings, agreed with him, and thought that this would happen at a time 'not very remote'.

This attitude towards Indian polity and culture was known as romantic, not because it romanticised or falsified the Indian situation but because its advocates were representatives in India of that philosophical reaction against 'the age of enlightenment' which was known as the Romantic Movement and led by S. T. Coleridge. The romantics and the Westernisers in India in fact represented two fundamentally different concepts of human nature and human society. From the 'age of enlightenment' with its mechanical model of the universe had developed utilitarian philosophy and *laissez-faire* economics, which insisted that the individual should be free 'to follow reason and the main chance',[19] and their conviction that this freedom would work out in 'the happiness of the greatest number'. Coleridge, on the other hand, revived in nineteenth-century terms the insights of the Cambridge Platonists, and declared that human society is not a mechanical assemblage of separate individuals, but a complex organic growth in which 'no man is an island' and all are 'involved in mankind'. The interaction of these two great schools of thought is of major importance in the developments of the

---

* By 1818 Lord Hastings had put down the Pindari brigands and brought much needed peace to large areas of central India. 'The ploughman', he wrote in February 1819, 'is again turning up a soil which had for many seasons never been stirred except by the hoofs of predatory cavalry' (quoted in Seeley's *Expansion of England*).

nineteenth century, and the Quakers whose encounters with India began during these years cannot be understood without a recognition of the intellectual climate in which they lived.

Many of the Quakers to whose dealings with India we shall now turn were affected by the currents of evangelical thought and the assumptions of *laissez-faire* philosophy. Awareness of the fundamental questions Coleridge was raising came only slowly, in the latter half of the nineteenth century. But for forty years before the Sepoy Mutiny a number of Quakers were becoming interested in Indian affairs. Some of these were merchants like James Cropper, who took advantage of the new trading opportunities after 1814. Some were philanthropists like William Allen, interested in the British and Foreign Schools Society. A few were ardent evangelical Quakers who urged the Society to send missionaries as others did; their pleas, however, were unsuccessful for many years.

The first Quaker interventions in India were a direct result of the part Quakers had played in the campaign to end slavery. The work for the slaves had been done in England, by fact-finding, publicity and pressure on the centres of power. When Quakers became aware of India's claims on their compassion they went to work in the same way. The first Quaker friends of India never saw India at all.

III

The British India Society
1815–1843

The principles of true politics are those of morality
enlarged.

Edmund Burke

In the autumn of 1815 a merchant ship named the *Bengal* dropped
anchor in the Hugli river off Calcutta at the end of her maiden
voyage from Liverpool. She had left England in May, when the final
struggle against Napoleon was at its height, and British merchant
shipping found it prudent to be armed against possible enemy
attack. Those who watched from the shore as the beautiful vessel
moved upstream saw that she too carried guns, but when they
boarded her they found that the 'guns' were dummies made of
wood. 'Yes,' explained the crew in answer to their wondering questions, 'them's Quaker guns. "Quakers" would be no use in a fight,
but they look all right at a distance. They frighten the pirates away –
and they cost much less than the real thing!'

The *Bengal* not only carried Quaker guns, she was a Quaker-
owned ship. As soon as the East India Company's monopoly was
ended in 1814, the Quaker firm of Cropper and Benson had had her
specially built for the India trade, and she continued in service till
the 1830s, after which sailing ships were gradually replaced by
steam. Many Quakers disapproved of 'Quaker guns' because they
were a form of deception, and James Cropper had other ships
sailing the Atlantic without them. He himself had a horror of
violence, but his crews were not all Quakers, and we do not know
what the pressures on him were.[1]

One of James Cropper's commercial interests was in East Indian
sugar, and one of his chief humanitarian interests was in ending
slavery. He became convinced that the best way to bring this about
was to enable sugar from India, grown by free labour, to compete on
equal terms with the slave produce of the West Indies. If the

unequal import duties which favoured the slave plantations were to be abolished, he argued, East Indian sugar would cost less than slave sugar, and slavery would disappear because it would be unprofitable.[2] Cropper urged these ideas upon Wilberforce in a series of 'Open Letters', but his personal involvement in the East India trade made it easy for the plantation interest to accuse him of selfish motives, and his proposals were not accepted. They were not forgotten, however, and they were later revived in another form.

During the years following 1815 a few obscure Quakers did actually visit India, but their very existence would be unknown except for a few scattered obituary notices.[3] The man who first aroused Quaker interest in Indian affairs was not himself a Quaker, though he had had Quaker connections from childhood.

This was the Cornish sea-captain, James Silk Buckingham, whose mother, Thomasina Hambly, was of Quaker stock, and who had learned from her and her friends to value Quaker standards of integrity and humane feeling. When at the age of twenty-one he took command of his first ship he introduced a humane and sensible discipline in place of the brutalities which were then so common. A year or two later, when the ship incurred some slight damage in a storm, he was too honest to co-operate with the owners in defrauding the insurance company, and so lost his job. Later, sailing the eastern Mediterranean, he gained an intimate knowledge of Egypt and a useful fluency in Arabic. Between 1814 and 1817 he paid two extended visits to Bombay as a 'free mariner' in the interests of Egyptian trade. In Bombay his appreciation of Islamic culture attracted him to Justice Erskine, and he also met public-spirited businessmen like the enterprising young Luke Ashburner and Zachary Macaulay's friends, the Babingtons.

In June 1818 Buckingham sailed up the Hugli to Calcutta in command of an Arab-owned ship with a cargo of Arab horses from Basra. (It must have been an interesting if gruelling voyage!) When he reported delivery to the owner's Calcutta agent, he was instructed to go next to Zanzibar for a cargo of slaves. Slaves? Buckingham's Quakerly humanism revolted. He was in a strange port, ten thousand miles from home, but he resigned his command on the spot, and wondered what he should do next. The Calcutta merchant John Palmer, 'universally respected, the friend of the poor', heard about the incident. Here, he thought, was a man of principle, experienced and adventurous, who might be an asset to the city. He approached the stranded sea-captain and suggested that there was scope in Calcutta for a good independent newspaper; would Buckingham provide one?

The time, in fact, was ripe for such an enterprise. Lord Hastings had recently abolished the press censorship which Wellesley had imposed, and had declared that he regarded the public scrutiny of public affairs as the 'natural right' of his fellow citizens. He himself encouraged Buckingham to undertake the new task. The *Calcutta Journal*, the city's first serious English daily, was launched in October 1818, and its 'public scrutiny' of affairs was an immediate success. The very first issues contain much that is suggestive. They anticipate James Cropper's argument for 'free-grown' sugar, and show concern about the practice of slavery in the Malabar region of South India. They comment with keen appreciation on the movement for humanitarian social reform led by Rammohan Roy and his newly founded Brahmo Samaj; they describe with equally keen appreciation a London Quaker's open and dignified stand for integrity in local government.[4]

Buckingham had met the great Rammohan Roy (who was to be known to later times as 'the father of modern India') very soon after his own arrival in Calcutta. With natural courtesy he had greeted the oriental scholar in Arabic, and had been much impressed by the perfect English in which he responded. Roy was himself 'giving respectful expression', through the press, to Indian opinion: he conducted a popular newspaper in Bengali and another in Persian, then the lingua franca of educated India. He and Buckingham worked well together.

The *Calcutta Journal* soon began to make witty and pointed comments on some of the shadier practices of the bureaucracy, and Hastings warned Buckingham that the Governor-General's Council, composed of senior officials, resented his criticisms. 'Don't set the Ganges on fire,' he said, 'my Council won't stand for it.' But Buckingham enjoyed setting the Ganges on fire in a good cause, and when Hastings retired in 1823 he suffered the consequences. One of the senior officials became Acting Governor-General, and used his temporary authority to show his disapproval of journalistic freedom. He charged Buckingham with 'inciting native rebellion', expelled him from the country, and reimposed restrictions on the press. Perhaps, in a sense he did not intend, the charge had some truth in it. Thomas Munro had observed the previous year that 'a free press and the dominion of strangers are things which are quite incompatible'.[5]

Indian leaders protested. Rammohan Roy closed down his Persian paper rather than submit to the Press Ordinance, and he, Dwarkanath Tagore and others challenged its legality before the Privy Council. The appeal failed, but a former Bombay merchant, Sir Charles Forbes, who had returned home and entered Parliament, strongly supported Buckingham when the matter of his deportation came before the House of Commons in 1824. Quakers were interested in the principle of freedom of publication, and one of them, Jonathan Backhouse, saw a good deal of Buckingham and his Indian friends.

Buckingham settled in London and started a new paper, the *Oriental Herald*, in order to keep Indian affairs before the public eye. Jonathan Backhouse enlisted the interest of other Quakers, including William Allen and Joseph Sturge, and the shipowners James Cropper and Robert Benson.[6] When Rammohan Roy landed at Liverpool in 1831, to give evidence before the Select Committee which was preparing for the revision of the Company's Charter, the Cropper and Benson families and other Liverpool Quaker merchants welcomed him to Britain.

In 1833, after the Slave Emancipation Act had been passed, Parliament took up the debate on the India Bill, and attention was called to the existence of slavery in India. This was broadly speaking of two kinds. In some parts of South India, especially Malabar, certain castes were bound to the soil as agricultural serfs and often barbarously treated.[7] There also existed a form of personal domestic slavery. In the bad years following the 1770 famine Sir William Jones had seen cargoes of children brought down-river to Calcutta and openly sold, and the story repeated itself with every local famine. Starving parents handed over their children to anyone who would promise to feed them and save their lives, and unscrupulous men profited by the parents' despair.[8]

In addition, there had been for many years a slave trade between Malabar and Mauritius. Lord Cornwallis attempted to stop it in 1789, but the law was evaded and the practice continued. Even before emancipation Mauritius had also begun to import labour from India under the form of contract known as indenture ('the cost was not half that of a slave') and by 1838 more than 25,000 people had been recruited. By that time Macaulay was in India in the Law Commission, and he drew up stringent measures to regulate emigration. At the same time an Indo-Portuguese gentleman, Thomas Boaz, returned to Calcutta from a visit to Mauritius and reported on the extent to which indentured labour had been recruited by fraud and by outright kidnapping, with the connivance of the police. There was a great public outcry, and William Wilberforce Bird, a younger cousin of the emancipator who was then on the Governor-General's Council, suspended all emigration and instituted a Committee of Inquiry, which included both Indian and India-born members. They reported against any renewal of the traffic, and proposed regulations which would make it too expensive to be profitable.

There was a parallel agitation in England, led by Charles Forbes and Thomas Fowell Buxton, who had piloted the Slave Emancipation Act through Parliament. Buxton was intimate with Quakers and had married into an influential Quaker family, the Gurneys. In 1837 he founded the Aborigines Protection Society 'to watch over peoples threatened by colonial or commercial dominance'. Among these threatened groups were the so-called 'hill coolies'[9] who were being sent from India to Mauritius, and when, early in 1838, it became clear that West Indian plantations were also beginning to get labour from India, a 'Natives of India Protection Bill' was introduced in Parliament in an attempt to regulate the traffic. Charles Forbes opposed it, calling it 'a bill for the extension of slavery'; he took the same view as the Calcutta committee, that indentured labour ought not to be regulated, but stopped. West Indian interests, however, were too strong for him.

Among Quakers the most active members of the Aborigines Protection Society were the well-known London physician Dr Thomas Hodgkin, and Jonathan Backhouse's cousin Joseph Pease of Darlington, who in 1838, in his sixtieth year, handed over his business affairs to his son in order to give his full time to the work. When Pease went to London he found that Sir Charles Forbes was even more concerned about the famine conditions in Upper India than about the problems of indenture, and the two men worked closely together.

Forbes[10] was a year or two older than Pease; he had gone to India at the age of sixteen to join his uncle's firm, and had lived for twenty-two years in Bombay, where he found his most intimate friends among liberal Indian merchants, Parsee, Muslim, Hindu. He made no secret of his preferences. 'The more I see of my own countrymen,' he told the House of Commons, 'the more I like the natives of India!' He had returned to England and entered Parliament in 1812, and taken part in the debates on the India Act in

1813. His speeches, then and during the years which followed, show how well he deserved to be known, as he was, as 'member for India'. He put his finger squarely on the issues which were to engage both Quakers and Indian national leaders for the next century and more.

'My object', Forbes declared in 1813, 'is to get the Company out of India as merchants altogether. It should wholly abandon . . . the monopolies of salt and opium, both great evils to the country.' The Company should concentrate on government, but 'natives should be admitted to a fair participation with Europeans in the honours and advantages of serving the State. I am very sure that the more the natives are known the more they will be respected.' The government too needed radical reform; 'the present system will always keep people overtaxed and poor'. He continued to reiterate these points, and protested vigorously against unfair discrimination against Indian textiles, sugar and shipping. 'If India were governed by an independent ruler,' he told the House in 1822, 'it would not submit to this inequality.' By 1838 he was reporting 'the general opinion' that the people were in a worse state than they had been a century earlier, and that they only listened to the recruiting agents of the sugar colonies because of their desperate poverty. The Company had failed to honour its *first* obligation: 'to watch over the welfare of the people'.

Forbes's belief that the sufferings of famine were exacerbated by the Company's own greed, neglect and misrule was supported by a weight of evidence. For at least ten years past, upright and experienced Company officials had been publishing the results of their observations. 'The people are taxed to the utmost pitch of extortion.' 'Villages which twenty or thirty years ago were in a flourishing state are now completely deserted; their riches have been mercilessly drained away.' It was an ancient tradition that village *panchayats* should store surplus grain in good years to tide their people over the bad ones. Now there was no surplus to store. 'The Company system, even in favourable years, keeps the people in a state of abject penury.'[11] In 1838 a Quaker writer, William Howitt, printed a summary of such evidence in a book called *Colonisation and Christianity*, and at the same time a young Englishman from Malabar, Francis Carnac-Brown, published an indictment of conditions there.

During the years immediately preceding 1838 Quaker philanthropists' attention had been concentrated on the grave abuses of the 'apprenticeship' system which had replaced slavery in the West

Indies. Joseph Sturge and a non-Quaker abolitionist named George Thompson[12] had visited the colonies, and at considerable personal risk had collected enough first-hand evidence of the evil to convince Parliament that the system should be ended at once. When this victory had been gained many of the same people rallied to the support of Joseph Pease, who on behalf of the Aborigines Protection Society set himself to 'discover and combat the causes of famine'. Inasmuch as faulty administration was one of them, he appealed to British public opinion to effect the necessary changes. 'There is no argument like matter of fact,' he would say, and he had the relevant chapters of *Colonisation and Christianity* reprinted and distributed as a pamphlet. Buckingham and Charles Forbes, Joseph Hume and other radical friends of India joined him, and Thomas Clarkson, now an old man, gave warm support.

The questions raised by Indian famines, however, were of far wider scope than the purposes of the Aborigines Protection Society. Would Quakers have done better to limit themselves to the abuses of indenture, which had been so ably and dramatically publicised by the citizens of Calcutta? Would the same pertinacity as they had shown with regard to apprenticeship, and the experience they had gained in fighting it, have enabled them to give affective support to Forbes's demand that indenture too should be altogether abolished? One cannot tell. The fact remains that after 1840 the anti-indenture campaign lost its momentum, the planters had their way, and the evil system persisted for another three-quarters of a century, until C. F. Andrews's investigations in Fiji and a new wave of public indignation in India combined to end it.

Slavery in India itself was so different from that of the sugar colonies that British Quakers simply did not understand it. They pressed for 'amelioration' of conditions as they had done in the West Indies earlier, and welcomed Wilberforce Bird's Act of 1843 which declared slavery non-cognisable at law. They did not realise how ineffectual such an Act was bound to be so long as the subordinate officials who had to implement it were themselves among the slave-owners. Malabar slavery was one of those things which, as John Malcolm had pointed out, can be changed only by society itself. Vestiges of it have survived as 'bonded labour' into independent India, and one or two modern Quakers have participated, under local Indian leadership, in society's attempts to root it out.

Meanwhile a number of Joseph Pease's supporters urged that his concern needed a separate organisation. 'The British Society for bettering the condition of our fellow subjects the natives of British India' came into being. The cumbrous name, soon shortened to 'British India Society', described its aims; like Wilberforce in his anti-slavery work, it disclaimed 'party or mercenary or sectarian views'. Both its secretary, Francis Carnac-Brown, and Buckingham, one of its speakers, had first-hand knowledge of India; Pease's daughter Elisabeth was an able assistant. Among the younger men attracted were a number who were later to play a part in the development of Quaker interest in India: John Bright and W. E. Forster, Brown's nephew J. M. Ludlow, Buckingham's former colleague Frederick Denison Maurice. Joseph Pease's passionate hatred of cruelty and oppression was the driving power; he could not bear to think that the poor should die of hunger while village fields reverted to jungle, and (as he put it) 'the fertile lands of India were in possession of the tiger'. W. E. Forster and another young Quaker enlivened one public meeting by suggesting in verse a more arresting name for the Society:

'Call it in order to gain notoriety,
The Tiger-expelling-from-jungle Society!'

The fact that Quakers allowed the British India Society to hold its first London public meeting at their own London headquarters at the time of the Yearly Meeting in May 1839 is a mark of the confidence which Joseph Pease's single-mindedness inspired. It is noteworthy that speakers at this meeting quoted Munro and Metcalfe, and appealed for just dealings with India as a land at least as civilized and enlightened as Britain; one may doubt whether the full implications of such arguments were understood, but the meeting may nevertheless be said to mark the first general recognition by British Quakers that India had claims on their attention.

The Society was also welcomed by Charles Forbes's Indian friends and their younger partners in Bombay. A group of them, headed by the distinguished Jagannath Sankar Sheth,[13] expressed their warm sympathy with the Society's aims. They did, however, question one phrase in its manifesto – it had appealed to the 'Christian feelings' of Britain: did that mean that it would proselytise? Forbes, who in 1813 had warned Parliament that 'there is no saying what uneasiness the admission of missionaries might create throughout India . . . the ignorant would think that government was going to interfere with religion', was in a position to explain to Pease how sensitive India was on this point. Pease at once had the ambiguous phrase removed. With his encouragement a supporting committee representative of all religions was formed in Bombay, and included among others Buckingham's old friends the Ashburners.

Other difficulties soon arose. It was not easy to keep clear of politics. Members of the Society held differing views about the Corn Laws, and about something which touched India more directly, the opium traffic. The East India Company controlled the production and processing of the drug in India, and auctioned it in Calcutta. Respectable Calcutta businessmen shipped it to the Chinese off-shore islands, Lintin and Hongkong, and from there it was smuggled into China by armed desperadoes in defiance of Chinese law. The Government of China, finding its protests ignored, at last took action to punish the smugglers and destroy the drug. In 1840 Britain declared war, on the pretext that her flag had been 'insulted'.

Joseph Pease denounced in strong terms both the unpopular opium monopoly and the shameful, dishonourable war. It was a shock to him to find that not all members of the British India Society shared his views. Some of the London merchants were profiting by the war to speculate in tea;[14] even some Quakers were unwilling to press *too* hard for an early peace. Pease lamented their conduct but refused to be discouraged. 'A man whose determination does not rise when difficulty increases is good for nothing,' he commented. When he found that the attitude of the London merchants was 'tainted with the leaven of expediency' he turned for support to the provincial towns of England.

It was then, on India's behalf, that he and his supporters revived James Cropper's argument that slave labour could not compete in a fair market with free labour. Lancashire's demand for raw cotton had enormously increased, and it was being supplied by the slave plantations of the USA. British India Society speakers argued that Indian farmers, given a fair deal, could compete successfully with the slave-grown cotton; in addition, as their prosperity increased, they would provide an expanding market for Lancashire textiles – and everyone would be happy! Had not free-grown Indian indigo, as early as 1830, driven the slave-grown indigo off the London market?

It is easy to pick holes in such arguments now. They were used by men who had never seen India, and who did not understand that the 'free trade' policies in which they believed would not necessarily benefit India, and that politicians would promote British rather than Indian interests if the two conflicted. No one asked *why* India should send her cotton to be woven in Lancashire, while her own weavers were being reduced to desperate distress by the influx of 'cheap' Lancashire goods.[15] No one asked *why* India should accept the British verdict that 'she can never again be a great manufacturing country'.[16] As for indigo, talk of their 'free-grown' indigo would have seemed a bitter mockery to the Indian peasants who were being compelled, sometimes by lawless violence, to accept the risks of cultivating it.[17]

Joseph Pease showed greater understanding in his cautious approach to the wealthy landowner and businessman Dwarkanath Tagore. Dwarkanath was Rammohan Roy's disciple and friend, his partner in social reform and a believer in the possibility of equal co-operation between Indians and Englishmen in the interests of India. But with him 'business was business'; his hard bargaining contributed to the miseries of the indigo cultivators; as supervisor of a Company salt agency he had enforced the monopoly regulations efficiently but with little humanity; he was involved, along with British merchants, in the highly profitable opium trade.[18] When Dwarkanath was being lionised by fashionable society in Britain in 1842 Joseph Pease told him plainly that a meeting between them would only be useful if it enabled them to find means of helping the *poor*. He made his attitude plain:

> We have no respect whatever for native Indians of rank and wealth who conceal, while moving in commercial and courtly circles, those miseries of their poor countrymen which it is their duty to explain and if possible get amended . . .

Dwarkanath invited George Thompson, on behalf of the Landholders Society, to return with him to Calcutta. After some hesitation Thompson accepted, and had a friendly welcome from the Indian press, which recognised his genuine concern 'for the most oppressed', but wondered what he had in common with Dwarkanath and the landholders. He did in fact spend a good deal of time helping Dwarkanath to deal with the legal problems of landed proprietors, but he also helped to inaugurate a branch of the British India Society in Calcutta.[19] It attracted a number of young Bengalis whose spirits had been fired by India's first modern 'nationalist' poet, the Indo-Portuguese Henry Derozio. Derozio had died young in 1831, but some of his Bengali friends were alive to the miseries of the peasantry and eager, for reasons which were by no means wholly selfish, to see a larger participation by Indians in public affairs, in the spirit of the 1833 Act. The British India Society, with Dwarkanath's backing, encouraged them to organise politically, and so sowed a seed which was to bear much fruit.

Nevertheless, when Joseph Pease died in 1846 it seemed that his brave campaign had ended in failure. Forty-five years later, in 1891, delegates of the Indian National Congress visited Britain. Pease's daughter Elisabeth received them in her home; her father's aims, she said, had still not been achieved, for the salt monopoly, the land tax, the recurrent famines still pressed heavily upon the poor. But on two counts his insight had been prophetic: the 'misrule' of India was a moral challenge, not to be met by any measures 'tainted with the leaven of expediency'; and the 'bettering' of the condition of the Indian people did depend on responsible care for 'the fertile lands of India'. Joseph Pease's patient, unrewarded efforts to help the Indian peasant were not wholly forgotten. In 1948, at a simple ceremony in the Friends Burial Ground at Darlington, a tribute of flowers was laid on his grave by representatives of the High Commission of newly independent India and the British India League. 'Among the servants of India', as the High Commissioner said in his message, 'Joseph Pease's name has its place.' In his day, it may be, it was not possible to serve India except by failure.[20]

IV

Some 'Honest Englishmen'
1843—1885

> Mr Bright looks at India like an honest Englishman,
> Anxious that England should do her duty there.
>
> Edmund Whitty, *History of the Session 1852–1853,*
> quoted in G. M. Trevelyan, *Life of John Bright*

Joseph Pease's successor as the spokesman of Quaker concern for justice in India was John Bright. His interest in India had first been aroused by Buckingham, who in 1833 had given a series of lectures in his home town, Rochdale, when Bright was twenty-two. After Buckingham's talk on India Bright proposed the vote of thanks, in what is said to have been his first public speech. A few years later he became an active supporter of the British India Society; as a Lancashire mill-owner he was specially interested in Indian cotton as a substitute for that grown by slave labour in the United States, and after he entered Parliament in 1843 he began to press for an inquiry into 'the obstacles which prevent the increased growth of cotton in India'. When Parliament refused, he persuaded the Manchester Chamber of Commerce to send their own investigator; his report, *Western India*, was published in 1851. It confirmed what Bright had already realised, that the prosperity of Indian trade could be secured only by a healthier *political* relationship between Britain and the Indian people. For him, as for Joseph Pease, this was a *moral* issue. 'The moral law', he declared, 'is intended not only for individual life but for the life and practice of States in their dealings with one another.'[1]

It might have been supposed that Quakers, who had insisted on the application of this moral law to the national policy on slavery, would have supported Bright as they had supported Joseph Pease. In fact they gave very little active support. Although by the middle of the century some Quakers were doing fine public work in their own localities, they still had to contend with what Joseph Rowntree in 1838 called 'the essentially monastic opinion that we might escape the spirit of this world by avoiding its more public duties'. Bright's attitude was more like William Penn's: 'Government seems to me to be a part of religion itself, a thing sacred in its institution and end'. Some of the most deeply religious of the Quaker leaders felt it their duty to warn him of the 'dangers' and temptations of the path he had chosen, and he answered them with courtesy and humility: 'I believe I am not moved by ambition or the desire for personal advantage. I feel a strong love of what is just and a strong sympathy with those who suffer. I endeavour to base our government and policy on morality and truth.'[2]

In all this Bright had the support of Joseph Pease's former Quaker assistant W. E. Forster. Forster had 'married out', and so was no longer formally a Quaker, but he still identified himself with these Quaker interests. His wife was the daughter of Dr Thomas Arnold of Rugby, and her brother William Delafield Arnold, a sensitive, honest young man, was in India in Company service. By the time he revisited England in 1853 he had come to the reluctant conclusion, in the words of his autobiographical novel *Oakfield*, that 'the magnificent work of civilising Asia through British influence is *humbug*'. Like his father, he believed that government should be an instrument of the moral law, and it seemed to him that in India the moral law was being broken. As Forster listened to him his interest in India was rekindled.

1853 was the year when a Parliamentary review of Indian affairs was once more due. In preparing for it, Bright had the assistance not only of Forster but of a number of other members of the former British India Society, including its secretary Francis Carnac-Brown. He was also supported by 'a small and unpopular minority' among the proprietors of the East India Company: Joseph Hume, George Thompson, and two or three other knowledgeable men who had lived in India. Through them he was also able to get into touch with the new political associations which had come into existence in India partly as a result of the work of the Indian branches of the British India Society in Bombay and Calcutta.

Bright had other direct contacts with India which had not been possible for Joseph Pease; there were business channels and there was the Indian press. The restoration of press freedom by Bentinck and Metcalfe in 1835, and the establishment of a regular mail service between India and England in 1838, encouraged new newspaper enterprise. The *Bombay Times* was launched by a group of

British and Indian businessmen, some of whom had had links with
the British India Society, and by about 1850 Robert Knight, one of
Bright's business acquaintances in Bombay, became closely associated with it. Through informants such as these Bright soon became
aware of the seriousness of Indian discontent.

As early as 1839 a Scots banker in Agra, who like Francis
Carnac-Brown had been born and bred in India and knew the
feelings of the people, had written to Joseph Pease, in words that
were to prove grimly true, that if nothing were done about India's
just grievances 'there will be retribution within twenty years'.[3] More
than ten of those twenty years had passed, and the burdens of
taxation and the provocations of racialist insolence were as great as
ever. The uneasiness caused by 'the rising enthusiasm for conversion'[4] has already been mentioned, and this was increased by the
neglect of the ancient languages of religion, Arabic and Sanskrit, in
the new Westernised schools, and by evidence that some government officials were not always impartial where Christian interests
were involved.[5]

Politically there were two main sources of resentment. A clause in
the India Act of 1833 declared that no native of British India should
be excluded from any position in the government of the country 'by
reason only of his religion, place of birth, descent or colour'. This
provision had raised high hopes in India, but they had quickly faded
– it seemed all too clear that the 'mild' English intended 'to keep all
positions in their own caste', and their attitude was compared
unfavourably with that of their Mogul predecessors, 'who used
merit wherever found'.[6] The second source of resentment was a
series of annexations of Indian-ruled States – Satara, Ihansi, Nagpur
– by methods which showed, in Forster's words, 'a criminal contempt for native customs and rights', and which were widely condemned by ordinary people as 'robbery'. British rule was *not* necessarily an improvement. 'The traveller may discern the boundaries
between the dominions of the East India Company and those of
native rulers', wrote the *Bombay Times* in 1848, 'by the superior
condition of the country and the people in the latter.'[7]

Such were the facts and, when the East India Company's Charter
was once more debated in Parliament in 1853, Bright therefore
warned the House that 'the people of India might be goaded into
insurrection by continued apathy to the mounting evidence of
oppression and misrule'. He proposed that the Crown should
assume direct responsibility for India, and that there should be 'a

very much wider employment in Government service of the most intelligent and able men among the native population'. His motion was defeated; the apathy continued; in 1857 'retribution', in the form of the Sepoy Mutiny, brought appalling suffering for many innocent people, Indian and British alike. The British press published completely one-sided reports of events, and whipped up an ugly outcry for vengeance upon India. The Quaker journals did speak out, then, about the 'manifold wrongs' of which British rule had been guilty, but the British public was in no mood to listen to them. When Lord Canning set to work in India to administer 'justice, not revenge' he was jeered at as 'Clemency Canning . . . puling, sentimental and Quakerlike'.[8]

During that terrible summer John Bright was a sick man. He had suffered greatly in 1854–6 for his outspoken opposition to the criminal folly of the Crimean War, and had fallen seriously ill. When he recovered, towards the end of 1857, he was re-elected to Parliament. He refused to condemn the Government, as some Quakers wished him to do, for using force to suppress the Mutiny, but he insisted again and again that Government, if it wished to retain any *moral* authority in India, should admit frankly that it had done wrong by its high-handed disregard of Indian custom. Bright urged that the territories which had been annexed should be *given back* to their rightful rulers. 'Reduce the army,' he said, 'encourage local initiative, appoint *at least* two or three Indians who have the confidence of the people to the Governor's Council in every Province.' He must have known that such proposals had no chance of being accepted in 1858, but he made no secret of his opinion, which he shared with the great administrators of the 1820s, that India had the right and should have the power to rule herself in her own way.

After the Mutiny it became in fact increasingly clear that the experience had confirmed the British in a general determination to 'maintain dominion' in India. The number of British troops, far from being reduced, was greatly increased; instead of local initiative and flexibility, there was a new emphasis on centralised, authoritarian 'efficiency', which ended any hope of preserving Indian political institutions in the way that Munro and Metcalfe had wished. It became more difficult for the conscientious local official, with an intimate knowledge of his district, to exercise the wise and compassionate initiative which had previously been possible. In the tragic and pathetic 'indigo risings' of 1860 many such officials supported the oppressed cultivators against the British planters, but as the years went on government circles also became infected by the general 'Anglo-Indian' dislike and contempt for Indians.

The Indian Reform Society, which had been organised for publicity in Britain, struggled on for a few years but could not raise even a minimum budget from a hostile or indifferent British public. Its last actions were to publicise the wrongs of the indigo cultivators[9] and to issue a report on the Upper India famine of 1860: *The Indian Famine: how we might have prevented it and how we may prevent another*. But although the Society had to be wound up Bright did not abandon his efforts. Against all odds he concentrated on the patient education of public opinion. 'I am supported by the hope', he wrote, 'that I am sowing some good seed in men's hearts and minds on great public questions, and that fruit may one day not be wanting.' In view of the authoritarian atmosphere he refused, in 1868, the invitation to become Secretary of State for India in the British Cabinet. 'I should have been unable', he explained, 'to carry out the policies I believe to be right.'

Instead, like Joseph Pease, he persistently raised the issues of human need. His 'fact-finder', John Dickinson, was a close friend of Sir Arthur Cotton,[10] the great water control engineer, and Bright joined his voice with theirs to urge (with no success) that Government should undertake water schemes to prevent famine rather than (from ambiguous motives) encourage the railway mania of the sixties. There was another disastrous famine in 1866 in Orissa, for which the criminal lethargy of the Government was widely held to be responsible. In 1877 a similar disaster struck the Deccan. John Bright spoke up in Parliament, linking the two events: 'You have the rain from heaven; you have the great rivers. Yet in ten years millions perish by famine which great engineers and men of character and experience say positively might altogether have been prevented.' The public outcry resulted in the Famine Code of 1880.

Bright worked hard to influence public opinion not only in Britain but also in India. In 1857 his friend Robert Knight had become the editor of the *Bombay Times*,[11] gave it an all-India coverage, and in 1861 renamed it *The Times of India*, a name it still bears. Knight had many other business interests, however, and three or four years later he decided to give up the editorship. He visited England to look for a suitable successor, and some time in the summer of 1865 a Quaker journalist, William Martin Wood, was appointed editor, possibly as a result of consultation with Bright.

Wood was then thirty-six years old. He was not a Quaker by birth; his family had for generations farmed land around Fadmoor in north-east Yorkshire, but his grandfather had settled in Scarborough as a corn dealer and grocer, and when Martin Wood was sixteen he was apprenticed to the grocery trade with a Quaker firm there, the Rowntrees. He struck up a friendship with an apprentice two years his senior, a Quaker boy from Sheffield named Joshua Hopkins Davy. He was already an eager reader, and Joshua encouraged him and stimulated his interest in public affairs. Meanwhile Martin's father had himself become a Quaker, and before Martin completed his apprenticeship early in 1852 he too applied for membership in the Society.[12]

Joshua Davy had gone back to Sheffield and started his grocery business and Martin, who had not yet decided about his own future, joined him there. He found Sheffield an intellectually stimulating place. The pioneer Sheffield People's College was offering young working people the chance of a liberal education, in an atmosphere of responsible freedom and mutual help, if they were prepared to work hard in their free time.[13] Joshua and Martin joined the classes, and Martin soon decided to stay on in Sheffield. He set up a modest grocery business, and in 1855 he married Joshua's charming sister Deborah. The marriage was short-lived; they had been together barely two years when Deborah died of tuberculosis – a killer disease in Sheffield then.

The young widower, still under thirty, began to occupy himself with freelance journalism, in company with James Wilson, a skilled grinder in the cutlery industry who was a leader in the Sheffield People's College. The two young men found ample scope for their talents, placing articles in the local newspapers which at that time were being established in many northern industrial towns. Politically Sheffield was a radical city, and John Bright was a familiar figure on its public platforms. It may well have been Martin Wood's Quaker connections and radical sympathies which led to his being invited, some time in 1861, to join the staff of a Quaker-owned paper, the *Lancaster Guardian*, which was a political supporter of John Bright.

This was a crucial decision; Wood handed over his shop to his brother-in-law Arthur Davy, and left Sheffield and the grocery trade for full-time journalism in Lancaster. There, and throughout Lancashire, the year 1862 held only one all-absorbing topic: the cotton famine. The American Civil War had blocked supplies, and there was widespread unemployment and distress. 'How shall we supply our cotton market?' asked scores of pamphlets. They all looked to India for the cotton, but they were concerned with Lancashire's welfare, not India's.

The *Lancaster Guardian*'s press published a pamphlet of a different kind: *Land in India: whose is it?* by Martin Wood. This focused on India's interests. To enable the Indian farmer to produce surplus cotton for the Lancashire mills, Wood declared, the land revenue must be used for *his* benefit, *his* security of tenure must be assured; the burdens on the Indian poor must be lightened by the abolition of 'the inhuman tax on salt' and 'the degrading revenue from the opium traffic'. Wood was of course writing at second hand, but he was dealing on Bright's principles with the larger, ethical issues. It is a possible conjecture that Bright saw the pamphlet, and put Martin Wood in touch with Knight about the opening in Bombay.

By 1865, however, Martin Wood was no longer in Lancashire. He had begun to work for a literary weekly in London, and had found time to matriculate and take a course in political economy at University College. He had also got to know two Quaker members of the former British India Society, Dr Thomas Hodgkin and William Howitt, and his increasing interest in India had been further stimulated by James Wilson, his former Sheffield companion. Wilson had gone to India in 1863 on behalf of his cutlery firm, and while there had been offered and accepted the editorship of the *Indian Daily News* in Calcutta. Martin was ready for a similar adventure. He accepted the Bombay offer, and a Sheffield Quaker woman of his own age, Lydia Milner, agreed to follow him to Bombay and become his second wife.[14]

For the next sixteen years Martin and Lydia Wood made Bombay their home; as time passed they were increasingly identified with the life of the city and of India. There, between 1867 and 1871, their three children were born. When, after nine years, Martin Wood reluctantly withdrew from *The Times of India* (apparently because of differences in outlook among the shareholders) he continued to live in Bombay and to 'educate public opinion' by freelance journalism. His contributions to Indian papers cannot be identified with certainty, though one may hazard the guess that certain vigorous comments by 'our Bombay correspondent' in James Wilson's *Indian Daily News* may be from his pen. In 1878 he launched his own independent weekly, the *Bombay Review*, which continued in circulation until the family left India in 1881. He himself regarded this as his best work; he felt that it reflected 'the riper experience of Indian affairs' which he had acquired in a dozen years of strenuous public life.

During his first years in Bombay Wood won respect by the steady common sense with which he countered the financial panic that followed the collapse of the inflated cotton market in 1866. The city was intellectually and socially alive. One of Elphinstone's first acts as Governor in 1820 had been to found a Native Education Association, and the Elphinstone College had been established in his name in 1827. By about 1850 some of its young graduates, led by Dadabhai Naoroji, were working for religious reform in their Parsee community and joining with Hindus like Jagannath Sankar Sheth in social and political activities. In 1867 the *Prarthana Samaj* ('Prayer Society') was launched; like the Brahmo Samaj it stood for social reform, but it avoided the sectarian spirit, and aimed at working as a leaven within society in the tradition of the Marathi saints. It attracted two of the greatest men of their time, R. G. Bhandarkar and M. G. Ranade. These men, and the Parsee journalist B. M. Malabari, whose special concern was the welfare of women, became part of the Woods' circle of friends.

Wood played an honourable part, along with Pherozeshah Mehta and other distinguished citizens, in the reform of Bombay municipal government. His main concern, however, was with the questions of all-India importance on which he worked with Bright. He repeated, in Indian terms, Bright's plea that Britain should 'not think of garrisoning India but of governing her' – with justice, with generosity and in a real partnership with her own people. 'No culture or training', he declared (in the spirit of Sir Thomas Munro), 'will ever raise a nation to real excellence except that which results in their taking a goodly part in the management of their own affairs.' He therefore welcomed the political awakening of India, and paid a generous tribute to Dadabhai Naoroji for the healthy national sentiment which he had aroused, 'free from bitterness and mere antagonism'. 'Political revivals', he wrote drily, 'are usually of far greater benefit to a country than those called religious.'[15]

Along with this defence of the aspirations of Indian nationalists went a passionate care for the sufferings of the poor. Martin Wood wrote in burning indignation (as did James Wilson in Calcutta) of the mishandling of relief measures during the Orissa famine of 1866. In article after article he condemned the 'pride and haste' with which railway building had been preferred to the proper provi-

sion and maintenance of irrigation and navigation works. One
hard-hitting editorial may be quoted:

> Only brave Sir Arthur Cotton had the clear-sightedness to raise
> the question, whether water was not better than iron. The people
> have railways given them instead of navigable canals; iron is
> brought from Europe in English ships, while India's iron is
> unutilized and indigenous intellect and talent are not trained;
> English engineers and surveyors plan expensive railways for
> which *the masses pay* – in a country whose first want is water. The
> natives of India are not fools because they are vegetarians – they
> are as clear-brained as our own race. They have their own opin-
> ion as to why we make railways and not canals. We should have
> acted very differently if we had allowed ourselves to consult the
> natives of the land and consider *their* needs. The people of India
> are entitled to be asked to decide what *they* want, and to have
> some say in how their money shall be spent.
>
> (The Times of India, 1873)

The masses pay. This was what most aroused Martin Wood's
anger and compassion. The poor of India paid not only for the
railway mania, but for a bureaucracy whose 'listless heavy heedless-
ness' was 'far more terrible in practice' (as in its heedless apathy to
forewarnings of famine in 1866) than the sporadic lawlessness of
which Indian princes might sometimes be guilty. It was most in-
tolerable of all that the poor paid, through the cynically inflated
'Home Charges' in the Indian budget, for things which did not
concern India at all. Wood asked why other journalists were silent
about this aspect of the budget – and answered his own question:

> Probably they fought shy lest they should be accused of 'medd-
> ling with politics'. That reproach has generally been flung at
> those who [attempt] to get justice done by a powerful class or
> country towards its subordinates or dependants – in this case, by
> England towards India.
>
> (The Times of India, 1869)

Martin Wood himself was of comparatively humble origin and
had spent much time among the radical artisans of Sheffield; he had
little sympathy with what he called 'our middle-class empire' and its
'civilising and christianising' mission. His early experience had

given him a great respect for 'ordinary' people, and a belief in their capacity for sound moral judgement, once they had understood what was involved in any public question. He was therefore indignant when it appeared to him that the Government of India was 'keeping the people in leading-strings' and denying them access to the authentic information 'which is essential to intelligent discussion'. He always insisted that the pros and cons of any controversial question should be placed before the public side by side, fairly and openly, and the human spirit *trusted* to recognise which way lay justice and peace.

'Civilisation', in Wood's view, was not something material which the British could import into India with the railways and the Manchester textiles. It was a spiritual matter, 'not to be induced from without but to be evoked from within'. He looked at India through the eyes of his Indian friends, and saw the value of ways of life which most Englishmen dismissed as 'uncivilised'. He pointed out, for example, that 'primitive' mud-built houses are cool and practical in the Indian climate, and that caste organisation 'is not the entirely evil thing that too eager reformers would have us believe'. We do not know how intimate he was with Mahadev Govind Ranade, but there are suggestive parallels in the thought of the two men. Ranade, like Wood, declared that true national growth must be 'evoked from within', 'spring from one's own essential past', although some creative idea coming from outside may help to call it forth. Ranade's words to a conference of social workers in Allahabad in 1892 might equally well have been spoken by his Quaker contemporary: 'The new idea needed is that of freedom, *responsible to the Voice of God in us*, a healthy sense of the true dignity of our nature and high destiny.'

Of the Woods' happy home life in Marine Lines, Bombay, no record remains, but among their close friends was a Quaker family named Lidbetter. Thomas Lidbetter was five years senior to Martin Wood and had had an adventurous life. He had gone to sea, become a master mariner, and after an eventful career had turned to shipbuilding. About 1860 he was employed in Karachi in the building of the Indus River Steam Flotilla. When the job was finished he stayed on in Karachi with his wife and little daughters, and went into the shipping insurance business with an Indian partner. Like other honest men they were ruined by the financial crash of 1866 and Lidbetter brought his family to Bombay and began to earn his living as an 'average adjuster'. He and Lydia Wood had been pupils at the same Quaker school (Ackworth) and the two families must have derived much comfort from their shared Quaker background. When the Woods' second son was born in November 1871 they gave him not only a family name, Arthur (for Arthur Davy), but also the name Lidbetter for their Bombay friends.

The rest is conjecture, but there were three other Englishmen with whom Wood worked for India after his return to England, who may already have been known to him in Bombay – Allan Octavian Hume, William Wedderburn and William Digby.

A. O. Hume was Joseph Hume's son, and was of the same age as Martin Wood. Although he had already entered East India Company service in 1849, when Martin was still a grocer's apprentice at Scarborough, and had become a District Officer at Etawah in Upper India, the parallels between his thought and Wood's are as suggestive as the parallels between Wood and Ranade. Hume has left on record how, as a boy in England, he was inspired by the Sheffield 'Corn Law poet', Ebenezer Elliott, and his moving hymn 'When wilt Thou save the people?':

> God save the people! Thine they are,
> Thy children as thy angels fair.
> From vice, oppression and despair
> God save the people!

Elliott had died in 1849, but his radical compassionate spirit was still very much alive in Sheffield when Wood went to live there in 1852, and in India both Wood and Hume did battle on the people's behalf against 'vice, oppression and despair', the one from outside, the other from inside the government administration. Hume's intimate knowledge of the mounting Indian discontent and frustration of the 1870s was behind his initiative in founding the Indian National Congress.

Hume worked closely on rural problems with William Wedderburn of the Bombay Civil Service. Wedderburn and Wood were friends in London, and it is likely that their common interest in the welfare of the poor had already brought them together in India. The same may be said of William Digby, who was editor of the *Madras Times* during Wood's later years in Bombay. Both men were deeply concerned about the Deccan famine of 1877 in which the Bombay and Madras Presidencies alike suffered heavily, and it is probable that the two independent journalists were in touch with one another in India before they began working together in Britain on behalf of the Indian National Congress.

John Bright and Martin Wood therefore played their part in the discussions and consultations which finally brought the Indian National Congress into being. The pioneer political leader Jagannath Sankar Sheth had died in 1865 before Wood reached Bombay, but he worked with Naoroji and Pherozeshah Mehta in his own generation and M. G. Ranade in the next. In his later years in England the cause of the Indian National Congress brought him into touch with two still younger men, Ranade's spiritual successor, N. G. Chandavarkar, and the man who emerged at the turn of the century as India's most able and selfless statesman – Gopal Krishna Gokhale. Gokhale, whom Mahatma Gandhi was afterwards to acknowledge as his own political guru, himself looked back in gratitude to all he had learned from the integrity and selflessness of Naoroji and Ranade. In this chain of public service the Quakers had their modest place. In 1885, when the Indian National Congress was about to be launched, Chandavarkar was one of those who visited England to publicise its aims. John Bright was the first man there to be consulted; he was an old man then, and the Indians were much touched by the warmth of his interest. 'No Englishman', they wrote, 'is more truly loved and respected by the Indian people.'[16]

V

Indian Initiatives:
Quaker Responses 1861–1864

The divers liveries they wear here makes them strangers.

William Penn, 1693

Reference was made in the last chapter to the parallel between John Bright and William Penn. Bright and Forster and Wood believed, as Penn did, that 'true godliness' must be concerned with justice and mercy in public affairs as well as in private; their work for India was part of a religious service to humanity. Like Penn, they were supported in what was often a difficult and lonely task by an inward assurance of upholding power – what Penn called his 'Rock'. But unlike him they rarely or never spoke of this deeper part of their lives. In their day an extreme religious reticence had taken the place of the eagerness of the first Quakers to seek out and respond to 'that of God' in men and women of other lands and faiths. Forster described his own saintly father, who was one of the heroes of Quaker service during the Irish famine of 1847, as one who 'had such an awful reverence for religion that it seemed to him almost profanity to speak of it all'. There were many Quakers like him.

Consequently we have no record or hint of any religious encounter between the Quaker families in Bombay and the Indians with whom they were on such friendly terms. Many of these Indian leaders were religious men; Naoroji and Ranade were widely known for their selfless and saintly integrity. While Ranade fed his spirit on the hymns of Tukaram, Martin Wood turned to the writings of the seventeenth-century English poet-mystics who were Tukaram's contemporaries. Perhaps they did find one another 'in that which is eternal'. The records are so scanty that an argument from silence is unreliable. We simply do not know.

Yet an Indian initiative towards religious fellowship with

Quakers had already been taken some years before Martin Wood settled in Bombay. It came from Calcutta and was presented to London Yearly Meeting in 1861 in dramatic fashion. When the members assembled for the first session Dr Thomas Hodgkin, ready as always to help in any Indian matter, asked permission to introduce two Indian visitors who had come to England as representatives of a Quaker meeting for worship in Calcutta. The request took the meeting by surprise; British Quakers had no inkling that any such group existed. It had in fact come into being entirely independently, and had no connection with any other Quaker meeting.

The story begins with the Indo-Portuguese or 'Luso-Indians', who were among the various communities of mixed blood which had grown up in the old European trading ports along the Hugli river. By the end of the eighteenth century Luso-Indians had settled in Calcutta in considerable numbers and were a respected mercantile community. Zealous Company chaplains and officials like Charles Grant were finding ways of encouraging Protestant missionary work in spite of the ban on British missionaries, and two churches were founded, the Old Mission Church, as it was later called, and the Lalbazaar Baptist Church. Many of their first adherents were Luso-Indians, and able members of this community provided much of the leadership. Two of them, Henry Derozio, the 'nationalist' poet, and Thomas Boaz, the leader of the Calcutta campaign against the emigration of indentured labour to Mauritius, have already been mentioned. By that time the Luso-Indians were using English as their mother-tongue and were often familiar with Bengali also.

Boaz was a member of the Lalbazaar Church, which in 1809 established the Calcutta Benevolent Institution to provide education for the poorer children of the Luso-Indian and other communities. The school grew so rapidly that in 1814 the Baptists asked Joseph Lancaster, the Quaker pioneer of the British and Foreign Schools Society, for a trained man to help them. Lancaster chose one of the ablest of his former students, a young man called James Penney, who reached Calcutta early in 1817 and stayed for the rest of his life. Penney was not a Quaker, but we may be sure that his reports to the Schools Society would be read by many of its Quaker supporters, and contribute to their interest in missionary work among those whom Penney called 'the perishing heathen'.

Penney's reports show that among the heterogeneous crowd of

children in the school ('Musalmans, Bengalis, Portuguese, Armenians, Jews') the Luso-Indians ('Portuguese') were in a large majority and that they set the pace. 'The Bengalis', Penney wrote, 'see that the Portuguese, by having a trifling acquaintance with English, obtain from the Europeans the most respectable situations as writers etc. . . . instruction to them is a medium to wealth.' It seems reasonable to conjecture that some of the future Quakers were educated in this school. There is no proof, but there is suggestive cumulative evidence. Quaker Luso-Indian names occur in the school records, and the jobs in which a number of the Quakers are known to have been employed are precisely of the 'respectable' type to which the students of the Institution aspired. Several Quakers had had Baptist connections; the initiator of the group, William Gomes or Gaumisse,[1] reported that he had been driven to seek for fresh light because he was repelled by the controversies about baptism which were going on about 1843. The Baptists practised 'believers' baptism' while other churches baptised infants, and their disputes involved, among other things, alternative translations of Bible passages which might be used to support one or the other side. In that context it is interesting that another future Quaker, S. Pir Baksh, was employed by the Baptist scholar Dr John Wenger on Biblical translation.

William Gaumisse found the fresh light he was seeking in some books which, as he put it, 'fell in his way' – books which he found, in all probability, on one of the numerous second-hand bookstalls of Calcutta. One of them was Robert Barclay's *Apology for the true Christian Divinity*, a vigorous exposition of Quaker faith written in 1676 by one of the ablest young leaders of the first Quaker generation. Gaumisse also found two more recent books: Thomas Clarkson's historical and descriptive *Portraiture of Quakerism*, and the *Memoirs* of Clarkson's British Quaker contemporary, Joseph John Gurney.

Amazing as it seems that the young seeker should have discovered these books and so found help in his perplexities, the fact that Quaker books were available in Calcutta is not in itself surprising. Many of the merchants and officials who travelled between Britain and India provided themselves with books to while away the tedium of the long voyage, which even in favourable weather took at least fifteen weeks.[2] Among these travellers were some Quakers. In 1840, for example, a young Quaker named Saunderson Walker reached Calcutta on a trading vessel belonging to his father's firm in

Gateshead on Tyne, after a journey which had lasted over five months. His journal is evidence of other Quaker links with the city. In it he described a Calcutta shipping agent with whom he did business as 'a pleasant moderate man with *still somewhat* of the manner and appearance of a Friend'. He also described how cheaply and easily good books could be obtained second hand – and how the book-sellers' touts would run alongside one's palanquin in the streets and thrust attractive volumes through the curtains. So it is easy to imagine how Barclay, or Clarkson, or Gurney might have found their way on to a Calcutta bookstall. What is not so easy to imagine is the impression they made on the young Luso-Indians who discovered them.

William Gaumisse and his friends were living in the midst of a great ferment of thought. The Calcutta of their youth, of the 1830s and 1840s, was a city where momentous new ideas were felt to be gathering strength. Bentinck and Metcalfe had restored to the press the freedom it had lost in the 1820s; the East India Company's government, urged on by liberal Indian opinion, had interfered with social practice to the extent of declaring suttee illegal; the rapid expansion of English education was revolutionising the outlook of many young people. Saunderson Walker, modest and observant and with a gift for making friends, recorded in his journal how young Bengalis took him to their homes and talked of the excitements and problems of 'great changes impending in their traditional society'.

Rammohan Roy, whose pre-eminence in the intellectual life of Bengal has already been mentioned, was the pioneer of this spirit of inquiry and reform. It has been well said that 'his was the modern secular temper in an Indian form',[3] and he raised basic religious questions. He had grown up in the centre of Muslim scholarship at Patna, and had learned from Islam a conviction of the unity of God which he found confirmed in the Sanskrit scriptures. Like the Sauds before him, he rejected idolatry and the belief in the sanctifying power of Ganges water; like the Sauds, and like the seventeenth-century Quakers, he refused to take an oath. He approached the Vedas as the Quaker Samuel Fisher had approached the Bible, believing that enlightened human judgement could and should discriminate between truth and error in traditional teaching. Later, when he himself studied the Bible, he was drawn to the story of Jesus, and urged that people of all faiths should accept Jesus's ethical teaching as 'a guide to peace and happiness'.[4] He regarded all those who obeyed 'that grand moral principle, Do unto others as you would be done by' as forming a spiritual community, a 'church of God' transcending sectarian boundaries. In answer to a question he quoted the New Testament: 'In every nation he that fears God and works righteousness is accepted of him', and added 'in whatever form of worship he may have been taught to glorify God'.

This rational ethical temper and inclusive outlook was unacceptable to most of the missionaries who were Rammohan Roy's contemporaries. They disliked his presentation of Jesus as a human guru rather than a divinely appointed Saviour, and they wounded him deeply by the harshness of their condemnation of Indian religious traditions. Rammohan on his part declared that there was much that was true and good in Indian beliefs and customs, and that the Christian faith in water baptism might be as irrational as the Hindu faith in the cleansing power of Ganges water. In 1861 a young man who had been influenced by his thought, Jagat Chandra Ganguly, was declaring in Calcutta that '*all* scripture is given by inspiration of God', and asking why he could not follow Christ without condemning the Hindu religion of his childhood.[5]

To people who were asking such questions the message of Robert Barclay came with the power and assurance of personal conviction. 'Not by strength of arguments', he wrote, 'came I to receive and bear witness of the Truth, but by being secretly reached by the Life.' He testified to 'an immediate inward revelation of God's spirit, shining in and upon the heart, enlightening and opening the understanding'. This, he said, is the True Light of which St John spoke, which enlightens everyone, including those who live where the outward Gospel is unknown. This 'holy pure Seed and Light which is in all', Barclay declared, is known by its power to call forth goodness; those who obey it 'feel themselves turned from the evil to the good, and learn to do to others as they would be done by, in which Christ himself affirms all to be included'.

Such words would reach the hearts of those familiar with Roy's ideas, and so would Barclay's teaching about the universal 'church of God'. The true church, he wrote, includes all those, 'both among heathens, Turks, Jews, Christians . . . of whatsoever nation or people they be', who 'become obedient to the holy light and testimony of God in their hearts, so as to become cleansed from the evil of their ways'. Barclay's testimony, however, included an experience of human fellowship which was largely absent from Rammohan's. Rammohan's reforming society, the Brahmo Samaj, was in his day coldly rational; it relied upon 'strength of argument'. Barclay, as he testified, had been reached *not* by argument but by a fellowship of loving friends who rejoiced in one another's company and together worshipped 'the Life', both in silence and in words of prayer or praise.

The warmth of this experience of togetherness glows through Barclay's pages; it seems to have captured the Calcutta seekers as Rammohan's more purely rational arguments could not do. Here was a faith which made possible a whole-hearted loyalty to the teaching of Jesus and to the light of the Spirit, untrammelled by the limitations and exclusiveness which the Calcutta churches imposed. One may imagine the group reading Clarkson's book alongside Barclay's and so learning the facts of the origin and history of the Quakers. In Joseph John Gurney's *Memoirs* they encountered a saintly spirit who loved the Bible and its message deeply, but knew also that 'the pure well-spring of life' must be sought by turning *inward*. Gurney, like many Quakers of his time, used the language of evangelical religion; at the same time he recognised the 'universal saving Light' outside Christian circles, for example in the teaching and practice of the Sauds, in whose 'Quaker-like' principles he was much interested.[6]

The group which was thus drawn to Quakerism was a mixed one. There were a number of 'East Indians' (as the communities of mixed blood were collectively called), including several Luso-Indian families, at least one of Dutch origin, and one with the English name Howatson. There were a number of Bengalis, some of them Brahmins, and some from various castes who had become Christians before they encountered Quaker ideas. S. Pir Baksh, a Muslim convert to Christianity, was associated with the group from very early days, although he did not commit himself fully until later. What is impressive is that these unknown 'seekers' cared so deeply for the Light they had received that for fifteen years or more they maintained their Quaker identity with apparently no further help or guidance than what they had found in their books.

It is possible that the plan to visit England in 1861 was made because circumstances provided the opportunity. The two who made the journey were a couple of Dutch descent, Mariano and Cecilia D'Ortez, whose family home was in the old Dutch settlement of Chinsurah. Mariano was a 'commission agent' in Calcutta, and it may well have been through his shipping contacts that he and his wife were able to work their passage to England as stewards or attendants on a passenger vessel. Once in England it would not be difficult to discover the Quakers.

What followed has been described as 'one of the most moving and dramatic incidents in the history of the Society of Friends'.[7] Mariano and Cecilia carried with them a letter of introduction from their fellow Quakers in Calcutta, and it must have seemed to them a simple, natural thing to ask the London body for admission and a hearing. To the Yearly Meeting the request was so novel and unexpected that the old Quaker habit of defensive withdrawal asserted itself, and instead of giving a warm welcome to those who had come so far with such a wonderful story they kept their visitors waiting all morning outside closed doors, while technical objections to their admissions were raised and overcome. Finally Thomas Hodgkin was allowed to bring them in, and their letter was read. It contained an appeal to British Friends for 'a Quaker missionary' to help the Calcutta group to grow in the faith. The appeal, like the visit, found London Yearly Meeting unprepared, and after about three weeks in England Mariano and his wife returned home, taking with them more Quaker books, but no assurance of the kind of help they most needed.

Help, however, was soon to be forthcoming. When the report of London Yearly Meeting reached Quakers in Australia two of them, Edward May and his brother-in-law Frederick Mackie, felt moved to respond to the appeal. They reached Calcutta in November 1862 and spent the next ten weeks doing all they could to help the group. They found, May reported, 'a tremendous openness for a spiritual, non-priestly Christianity'. Thirty or forty people were attending the meetings, ten or twelve of whom regarded themselves as fully committed Quakers. May and Mackie accepted them as such, and showed them how to maintain the customary Quaker records. They also discussed with them the Quaker social testimonies, such as the refusal 'to fight with outward weapons', which aroused much interest. What would Quakers have done during the Sepoy Mutiny? asked the Indian students. What were they doing in the American Civil War which was then in progress? May and Mackie established a fruitful dialogue; one wonders what the outcome might have been if such contacts could have been maintained, but for Australia distance and cost made it impossible for the Australians to repeat the visit, and other openings, as we shall see, were not followed up.

In January 1863, before the Australians had left Calcutta, a party of three Quakers arrived there from Britain. The leader was an elderly Friend named Russell Jeffrey, who for nearly twenty years 'had felt a leading to visit the peoples of India in the love of the Gospel'. The appeal from Calcutta had made him feel that the right time for the visit had come, and London Yearly Meeting endorsed his concern. It was arranged that two younger Friends, Henry Hipsley and William Brewin, should accompany him.

The outlook and interests of Russell Jeffrey's party differed widely from those of the Australians. May and Mackie had visited Calcutta solely in order to respond to the needs of the Quaker group, but for Jeffrey the group was only a minor and incidental part of his mission to 'the peoples of India'. This was planned on an elaborate scale; after spending five weeks in Calcutta the Quakers carried out an extensive tour of the country which lasted for over a year. They brought with them introductions to the Viceroy, some senior officials, and the leaders of the foreign missionary community; they seem to have had very little contact with Indian people except through these foreign agencies.* Their message was given mainly by preaching in mission churches or at gatherings arranged in the schools and other mission institutions which they visited.

Jeffrey and his party in fact belonged to the evangelical wing of London Yearly Meeting, and were ill fitted to respond to the questions which exercised the Indian Quakers. They had no sympathy with Barclay's or Rammohan's vision of a 'church of God' which transcended religious labels. Like most missionaries they condemned Indian religious practices as something they '*knew* [!] to be offensive to God'. They shared the belief that Britain's duty in India was to 'civilise and christianise' the population, and they therefore took every opportunity to urge government officials to adopt William Allen's *Scripture Lessons for Schools* (whose preface declared uncompromisingly that 'this book has God for its author') as a textbook in government institutions.

They did indeed maintain the traditional Quaker 'testimony' against water baptism, and during their first weeks in Calcutta they expounded it in a way that was embarrassing to the missionaries in

---

* An exception was their meeting with Dwarkanath Tagore's son Debendranath, the leader of the Brahmo Samaj. The exchange appears to have been little more than formal courtesy, for their religious interests were remote from his. A quotation will illustrate his position:

> We must hold up as a beacon the highest truth of the Hindu Shastras. In their light we must purify our heritage of custom . . . but we must beware of proceeding too fast in matters of social change, lest we be separated from the greater body whom we would guide and uplift (*Autobiography*, p. 152).

whose churches they spoke, for Indian audiences eagerly 'laid hold of the fact that there are good Christians in the world who have never been baptised'.[8] The missionaries complained that the Quakers were injuring their work, and Jeffrey and his friends found themselves in an ambiguous position. Basically they shared the missionary outlook, and agreed that Christians ought to separate themselves from their old associations (even though not by baptism). From then on they ceased to lay stress on Quaker peculiarities, and discouraged inquirers. Some educated young men, who had attended their early public meetings, came and told them that they were 'ready to form themselves into a body' to follow Friends' principles. Jeffrey advised them 'to move cautiously', and did *not* introduce them to the existing Quaker group, as would have seemed the natural thing to do.[9]

Although the British Quakers conscientiously attended the Calcutta Meeting for worship and visited the homes of its members, it is clear that they were not at ease among them. The social barriers were as great as the divergence of ideas. Jeffrey's social connections were with judges and other high-ranking officials of the administration. He and his party moved naturally in the upper levels of British society, and in those years after the Mutiny the British in India maintained a social hierarchy among themselves and a social distance from the native population ('East Indian' and 'Indian' alike) which made natural relationships very difficult. It is significant that the only English Quakers who were able then to overcome these barriers were a couple of brothers, Benjamin and William Hayllar, who arrived in Calcutta later in 1863. The Hayllars were British working men, and were among those temporarily employed as 'guards' on the new East Bengal Railway to train their East Indian counterparts. They could find common ground with the Calcutta Quakers, who were themselves in the main employees, and so long as they remained in the city they were regular members of the Meeting. Jeffrey and his companions, on the other hand, were 'made strangers' by what William Penn would have called the 'divers liveries' of their very different social and cultural background.

It has been plausibly suggested[10] that the British Quaker visitors hesitated to suggest that London Yearly Meeting should form any closer ties with the Calcutta Friends because they regarded them as 'poor and insecure', and therefore a possible financial liability! If that was so, it shows how little they understood the position. Every member of the group who can be traced had secure employment and, by Indian standards, a modest competency; it is likely that Mariano and Cecilia D'Ortez were not the only ones who owned family property.

During the years covered by this chapter two divergent trends in British Quakerism were in operation. The one which was most visible and immediately most relevant for India was the growing pressure for the Society to abandon its original insights (so many of which were described in Barclay's *Apology*) and to identify itself with the outlook of evangelical Protestantism. The result was the beginning in the 1860s of a Quaker foreign missionary society.

The other trend remained, for a long time, 'underground' and almost invisible. Its re-emergence can be dated symbolically from two books published in 1859. One is famous: Darwin's *Origin of Species*. The other was a prize essay, *Quakerism Past and Present,* by a young Quaker called John Stephenson Rowntree, which inquired why Quakers were then apparently a dying sect. Darwin's book, and the intellectual ferment which followed it, was to renew for Quakers the challenge to 'experimental' religion and all that it implied. Rowntree's book was the first fruits of an equally significant influence, that of the social thought of Coleridge and his successors, who were the heirs of the Cambridge Platonists.

A generation was to pass after 1859 before the second trend made any visible impact upon the public life of the Society of Friends. Meanwhile the two trends mingled and blended in the thought and experience of individual Quakers in India as in Britain. There was no one pattern, no uniformity, even in the work of the missionaries to which we now turn.

VI

Benares and Beyond 1864–1872

It is hard to distinguish proselytism from evangelism,
and so (in rejecting proselytism) we are tempted to
neglect evangelism. We speak too little of what Christ
has done for us.

H. G. Wood,
'Letter from Tambaram' (India) in *The Friend*, 1939

Russell Jeffrey and Henry Hipsley were representative of a considerable body of Quakers who shared the belief in Britain's 'civilising
and christianising' mission in India, and regarded the direct British
rule which was established after the Mutiny as a renewed opportunity both for the extension of commerce and 'still more for the
spreading of the Christian religion'.[1] During the 1850s the work of
David Livingstone, who combined missionary enthusiasm with a
concern for slavery in Africa, had caught the imagination of many
Friends, who urged, as some had been urging ever since 1830, that
Quakers ought to take up missionary work themselves.

In 1859 this concern was expressed in moving terms by George
Richardson, whose nephew Saunderson Walker had kept the
record of his voyage to India in 1840 from which we have quoted.
Richardson had seen the young man off when he sailed, and no
doubt questioned him closely about his experiences when he came
home. It seemed to him that Quakers were neglecting an important
part of their religious calling. In 1859 he was eighty-six years old,
but he wrote no less than sixty long personal letters to influential
members of the Society, in which he pleaded that Friends should
labour not merely 'to improve men's temporal condition' but 'to
turn their minds to God'.

This is a constantly recurring theme in Quaker history. It is as old
as George Fox himself, who commented that 'your bestowing of
outward things to such as stand in need is the least love, and things
of little value in comparison to the things that are above and
immortal'.[2] George Richardson's letters, some of which were pub-

lished in Quaker journals, made a deep impression. By the time Russell Jeffrey and his party returned to England in 1864 there were many Quakers who were ready to organise a Friends' missionary society. There was not complete unity, however. The Society, like all established bodies, had its quota of plain human inertia, and those who disliked change had specious arguments for doing nothing.* Others had more serious objections. For the missionary enthusiasts, 'turning men's minds to God' did not mean so much 'directing men to the grace and spirit of God . . . in their hearts'; it meant teaching them about the Biblical revelation and Christian doctrine. More 'old-fashioned' Friends feared that this could lead to spiritual pride. 'They tread on slippery ground', they said, 'who assume the capacity of giving *religious* instruction.'[3] Because of this difference of opinion London Yearly Meeting took no official action, but it permitted the enthusiasts to organise an autonomous Friends Foreign Mission Association (FFMA). The FFMA declared its aim to be 'to aid the spread of the gospel of our Lord Jesus Christ', and in India the first step towards this was taken in co-operation with the Church Missionary Society (CMS) in Benares.

Russell Jeffrey and his party had visited Benares, and after their visit a CMS missionary, Mrs Leupolt, wrote to appeal to 'wealthy Friends' for money to buy sewing-machines and pay a teacher for an industrial school for girls. In October 1864 her letter was published in the Quaker periodical *The British Friend*, where it was seen by an expert seamstress, a Quaker in her mid-thirties named Rachel Metcalfe. To her the appeal came as a call from God.

Rachel Metcalfe was one of those Quakers of humble origin and limited means who took little or no part in the affairs of the Society outside their own locality. Her Meeting at Macclesfield, however, had sometimes been visited by travelling Quaker 'ministers', some of whom had made her dream of possible missionary service. But her parents had died when she was still young, and for years she had had to work hard to support younger brothers and sisters. She continued to attend occasional missionary meetings, where appeals were made for 'the idolatrous, priest-ridden people of India', or for Livingstone's work in Africa. Africa attracted her, India did not.

* James Cropper wrote scathingly about the excuse that missionary work would be 'a hireling ministry': 'The love of the comforts of this world so prevails among us that it would be difficult to find members of our Society willing to make the sacrifices those do who are called by some of us hirelings' (letter to J. Sturge, March 1831).

Then in 1856 came 'a direct call of the Lord to India'. She herself
has preserved an account of how she felt. '*India?* It filled me with
dismay. Oh *why* Lord? I pleaded, but only with this response. Not
yet but in ten years. Time passed on . . . and I almost began to think
that the Lord might have other work for me. Then the call came
again. I simply waited for the way to open. Yet I often pleaded not
to go alone.'⁴

It is not surprising that in these circumstances Rachel should have
seen in Mrs Leupolt's letter the opening of the way, even though in
fact Mrs Leupolt was asking for money, not for personal service.
Rachel consulted Jeffrey, who advised her to follow Quaker practice and lay her concern before her local Monthly Meeting. The
Meeting refused to support it – Quakers no longer expected that
working women might be called to 'publish Truth' as they had done
in the early days of the Society. Rachel was not a recognised
'minister' and she herself knew that her concern was unusual. 'Mine
will not be a service such as we usually expect from Friends,' she
wrote (i.e. a preaching tour like Jeffrey's), 'but a *dwelling among
them*, teaching and helping in the daily routines of life.'⁵ It was a
Quakerly attitude, but at the time it was not generally acceptable.

Rachel, however, was sure of her 'call', and she won Henry
Hipsley's support. Hipsley was convener of the new FFMA committee, which somewhat grudgingly agreed to make it possible for her
to reach Benares – at the minimum expense to them! Rachel sold up
her modest assets and provided her own outfit and equipment; she
worked her passage to India as companion-help to a missionary
family, reached Benares with a few rupees in her pocket, and began
'helping in the daily routines of life' from the very day of her arrival.
It was November 1866, and just ten years had passed since her
mysterious 'call to India'.

Mr and Mrs Leupolt soon realised what a treasure they had got.
Appreciative letters describe Rachel's 'happy cheerful temper', her
technical skill and quick intelligence, and the zeal with which she
'threw heart and soul into her work'.⁶ She had a happy knack of
making friends, and in spite of difficulties of language her pupils
quickly gave her their confidence, and enjoyed talking over their
hopes and problems. Rachel enjoyed it too; she was 'dwelling
among them' on terms of equality and trying (as she wrote) 'to show
forth Whom I wish to serve in the little daily occurrences of life'.

She was less happy about other aspects of the mission – the
emphasis on preaching, and particularly the economic dependence

of converts; she longed to 'encourage young women to support themselves instead of hanging on to the missions'. She was uneasy in the class-conscious white society in which missionaries then moved. She didn't fit, and didn't want to fit. 'I have no wish to aim at the position others occupy,' she wrote. 'I prefer my own simple mode of dress and living with its fewer cares.' After she had been about eighteen months in Benares she therefore wrote to ask whether Friends would support her in an independent venture, and appealed for a married couple to share it with her.[7] She had no cut-and-dried plans. 'The way may open as we go step by step,' she said, but she did hope to use her special skills to run an industrial school of her own. The response to her appeal came not from Britain but from America. Elkanah and Irena Beard of Indiana Yearly Meeting volunteered to join her.

Elkanah Beard was a leading spirit among younger American Friends. He had refused to fight in the Civil War, but he had gone about the battlefields giving what help and comfort were in his power to sufferers on both sides. He 'feared neither God nor man nor devil', said the soldiers. Such was his reputation for integrity that the commanders of the rival armies had both authorised him to go freely where he wished; he was said to be the only man in America who could cross the fighting-lines unhindered. He needed all his toughness when after the war he and Irena organised schools for newly emancipated blacks in Mississippi and Louisiana, in areas where they were in constant danger of murderous attacks by bitterly resentful whites.[8]

The Beards had long felt an interest in India, and British Quaker visitors to the United States told them of Rachel Metcalfe's appeal. Elkanah's name was already known and respected among British Friends, and he and Irena were readily accepted for missionary service. They left London for Benares in the early autumn of 1869.

In 1866 Rachel had travelled via Calcutta, and this was still the simplest route. In Calcutta was the group of Indian Quakers, eager for spiritual support. It seems strange that neither in 1866 nor in 1869 was there any attempt to introduce the Quaker missionaries to them. Rachel, with her simple social background and knack of making friends, might have come much closer to them than Hipsley and Jeffrey had been able to do, and the contact would surely have been welcome to Rachel herself, who had 'pleaded not to go alone' to India. Apparently the FFMA did not consider the link important, and they arranged for the Beards to travel via Bombay, a shorter but more difficult route. They had to go by train from Bombay to Nagpur, then from Nagpur to Jabalpur by the horse-drawn mail-coach. From Jabalpur onwards to Benares was a recently opened railway whose surveyors had been exposed to attack from the insurgent bands – remnants of the Mutiny – that roamed the central Indian jungles.[9] The scars of the Mutiny, in fact, were still fresh; at each stage of the journey the Americans were shocked to find how much fear and hatred poisoned the atmosphere, and how many British people treated Indians 'as if they were unworthy of kindness or respect'.[10]

The Beards were also distressed to find how often Rachel herself was treated in missionary circles 'more as a servant than an equal'. Elkanah agreed that a new start was called for. 'The missionaries in Benares want us to go elsewhere,' he reported, 'and since becoming acquainted with them and their way of working we are quite of the same opinion!' To leave Benares altogether, he felt, would be too much like running away; but they might leave the mission settlements, and the unsavoury cantonment, and make their home in the real Benares, the Indian city.

This plan was carried out, and it says much for the confidence which Rachel and the Beards inspired that within a very few weeks of the Beards' arrival Indian students were helping them to find a house. One was actually offered them free of charge and for as long as they wished; it was not, however, quite suitable, and after a little search another was found on the high bank overlooking the Ganges at Prahlad Ghat. 'We could have had a house easily if we ate no meat,' reported Elkanah, 'and Paul would not eat meat if it made his brother to offend – but we are not *quite* ready to be wholly vegetarian.' A trivial comment perhaps, but one that shows a respect for Indian feelings very different from the contemptuous attitude towards vegetarian 'superstition' shown by some of their contemporaries.

Benares was an educational centre, with an old-established government college and another founded by its public-spirited Maharajah. There was the same ferment of thought as in Calcutta, and the same suspicion of missionary motives. 'Hindus are unable to see anything but a *political* motive in the vast mission outlay,' wrote a perceptive British observer who visited Benares and met the Quakers in 1870.[11] But once suspicions were overcome there was much friendliness, and many were attracted to the Quaker home at Prahlad Ghat, which might fairly be described as the first 'Quaker Centre' in India.

Rachel was already much troubled by rheumatism, and was never able to realise her dream of an industrial school, but even before the Beards arrived she had developed a keen interest in more general educational needs. She and Irena concentrated on helping the women and girls who were their neighbours to become 'better wives and mothers' – an aim which was to be central in all Rachel's future work. They soon had a school with as many pupils as they could manage, and more invitations to Hindu and Muslim homes than they had time to accept.

This work was stimulated by Rachel's friendship with 'Bessie' (Elizabeth Rebecca) Alexander, who was one of a number of Quakers who have lived almost unknown in India and done some modest but useful piece of work. She was ten years younger than Rachel; she had missionary interests and ample private means, and was living in Agra at her own expense and conducting schools for boys and girls. She may have been eccentric in some ways, but she seems to have had plenty of common sense, and she and Rachel exchanged visits and ideas.

It was Elkanah's work, however, which gave the Benares home its 'Quaker Centre' flavour. 'Tough' he might be, but he was deeply religious, and eager to share the joy he had found in the Gospel. In that he agreed with the missionaries, but his approach was so different that people wondered, he reported, whether these Quakers were deists. He was quick to appreciate the truth and goodness in Indian faith – in the beauty and dignity of Islam, and the simple sincerity of Hindu ritual worship on the river *ghats*. 'The grace of God is shining in many hearts,' he wrote. He welcomed the growing influence of Keshab Chandra Sen, now the leader of the Brahmo Samaj who was using it to preach a personal devotion to Christ which should be lived out within the framework of Indian culture, not by joining a separate sect. And, although Beard was not blind to the darker aspects of the 'priest-ridden' popular religion, which often 'oppressed his spirit', he was sure that 'God has not left the people without a witness in their own hearts concerning his love'.

Elkanah judged religion by its fruits in life. He defined idolatry in ethical terms as 'what is impure in imagination and wicked in practice'; salvation for him meant growth in goodness, in a life filled with 'the beauty of holiness'. People responded. 'This man must be sent of God,' they said, 'he is so full of love.' Students gathered in informal Bible-study groups, commenting on 'how nicely Jesus puts things'! Older men found comfort in Elkanah's readings from St John's Gospel. Arabic scholars from Lucknow sought him out, and Brahmin pilgrims from Bombay. A Rajah 'from west of Allahabad', whose three sons were studying in Benares, came to invite the Quakers to live in his territory and teach the people there. But at that time they had no thought of leaving Benares. Life in the city was too full and too challenging.

The Quaker home was visited also by many simple people and by some who were sick. For these the Quakers were able to claim the help of their most intimate friend among local Indian Christians, Dr E. J. Lazarus. Dr Lazarus belonged to a well-known Calcutta family of Indian Jewish origin; besides his dispensary he ran a printing press and was active in public affairs.[12] Both Rachel and the Beards owed much to his practical helpfulness, and it was possibly through him that Elkanah became aware of the great need for medical service, which he later urged upon the FFMA.

'People say', Elkanah commented once, 'what a solemn thing to die; but *I* say, what a solemn thing to *live*, a day at a time, for the social, moral and religious development of this people.' Tracts about death and a future judgement, which offered 'salvation' as a means of escaping punishment, did not seem to him to speak to the real needs of the common folk. The religion of the Gospels was not, he thought, divorced from the social and moral aspects of life. He therefore prepared a series of *Good Words*, attractive handbills carrying two or three sentences each: some of Jesus's parables of daily life, some of the Beatitudes, the 'two great commandments', the saying that God seeks to be worshipped in spirit and in truth. Dr Lazarus got the leaflets printed in Hindi and in Urdu, and they were widely used.

This was not all. Elkanah had a microscope, a source of unfailing interest among students, and he did his best to encourage and satisfy their natural curiosity in other fields also. He got them English and American periodicals and discussed the news with them. 'Why do Christians fight so much?' asked the young men as they read of the Franco-Prussian war; Elkanah's tales of his own experience in the American Civil War led to discussion of Quaker ideas of non-violence, justice and service.

The 'Quaker Centre', however, was short-lived. Before a year had passed both the Beards had been seriously ill, and Rachel's rheumatism was worse. It was decided that they should move to the healthier climate of Jabalpur, where Elkanah, hard as he found it to

leave Benares, hoped he might do similar work. He wanted especially to help those who confessed themselves disciples of Christ but
for honourable reasons felt they could not be baptised. These hopes
were shattered by Irena's continued ill health; the doctors said that
to stay in India would be to risk her life. The Beards left early in
1872, while Rachel remained in Jabalpur. It was a sad parting.

Five years later, with recovered health, the Beards once more
volunteered for service in India, where in 1877 a mature married
couple was needed. The FFMA did not appoint them. No reasons
were recorded, and Elkanah's letter, in which he is said to have
'explained his views', has not (contrary to custom) been preserved.
We are left guessing.

It is clear, however, that Elkanah's 'views' and those of the
leaders of the FFMA diverged to a considerable extent, even in
1870. For them, 'the operation of the Holy Spirit' was limited to
'true believers'. They saw nothing but 'a debasing superstition'[13] in
the ritual on the *ghats* which moved Elkanah by its sincerity. They
regarded Keshab Chandra Sen as 'outside the kingdom' because he
was not formally a Christian. They criticised Elkanah's handbills of
Good Words for omitting to preach Jesus as 'Saviour', and told him
that if he met with so little opposition from the 'heathen' he couldn't
be doing much good! (He replied, whimsically, that he had met
plenty of opposition from the *missionaries*!) Perhaps, even if there
had been no health problems, the plans for Jabalpur might not have
been approved.

Nearly fifty years were to pass before the next Quaker Centre
came into being in Calcutta in 1919. It was a response – too late – to
the invitation which Calcutta had sent in 1861 and which had been
so often brushed aside. If Elkanah Beard could have gone to *Calcutta*, how different the story might have been!

In 1872 Rachel Metcalfe, alone and increasingly infirm, reported
to London with quiet courage that 'the long dreary prospect before
me does not lessen the assurance that my coming to India was a right
thing'.

VII

Quaker Missionaries 1873 – 1901

> To organise – this is the paradox and dilemma, most
> deeply difficult for a movement whose essence is the
> breath of the spirit of God.   W. E. Hocking,
>
> *A Laymen's Report on Foreign Missions,* 1933
>
> Where is the frontier between missionary zeal and the
> will to power?
>
> Paul Tournier, quoted in *The Friend* (1978), p. 1279

The title of this chapter will probably seem a contradiction in terms
to many of those who have known Quakers in India through their
various projects and community service activities. 'Quaker *missionaries*?' they will say. 'But Quakers don't proselytise, they don't
preach their religion, they don't try to convert anyone to Christianity. They express their faith through their service and their friendships, and they very rarely put their beliefs into words.' This is
largely true of those Quakers who have been most widely known in
Indian public affairs during and after the struggle for independence.
But it has not always been true; it is still not true of all Quakers in
India. There have been, and there are, Quaker missionaries, men
and women who believe themselves called not only to live in the
spirit of Christ but to tell others of the joy and peace they have
found in him.

   The popular, unflattering picture of a missionary as a mere pro-
selytiser is a caricature of the truth. Unfortunately, as has been
pointed out in previous chapters, much harm has been done by the
arrogant condemnation of Indian religion of which too many missionaries have been guilty, but that is only part of the story. At the
heart of the evangelical missionary movement is a loving devotion
to Jesus Christ. In the lives of the greatest missionaries, like the
beloved Daniel Corrie,[1] this devotion expressed itself in a courtesy

and humility of bearing which won the respect and affection of *all* religious groups. Such men drew India to Christ, though not to organised Christianity. They were the forerunners of twentieth-century missionaries like C.F. Andrews. Elkanah Beard was in this missionary succession; he was eager to make the story of Jesus known, but he was too vividly aware of the social disruption involved in outward 'conversion' to try and make 'proselytes'. Rachel Metcalfe too had her roots in the older Quaker tradition and was much more ready to 'let her life speak' than to preach.

The FFMA, however, was controlled by men who believed, in common with other missionary societies, that the missionary's task was to make converts and to build them up into a separate Christian church. The secretary was an energetic young businessman named Henry Stanley Newman. Like many other evangelical Quakers he was as enthusiastic for 'Home Missions' in the dark underworld of England's industrial slums as for foreign missions in India. He and the members of his committee believed that the people they were trying to help needed 'a simple and pure Gospel', and that the distinctive forms of Quaker religious experience would not be of much use to them. 'You can't make Quakers out of these poor ignorant people,' said Robert Alsop at a conference in 1869. He was speaking about Home Missions, but the FFMA missionaries took the same attitude in India. 'It is not thought necessary', they reported, 'to insist on a complete understanding of the distinguishing views of Friends.' They wished their converts to be 'not a narrow sect, but part of the Christian church'.

The FFMA therefore did not insist that all its missionaries should be Quakers; a number of them came from Baptist, Presbyterian and other churches, and had no knowledge of Quaker traditions. In India, the Indian paid staff were recruited from the older Protestant missions. The criteria for membership in the 'Quaker church' which they built up were almost wholly doctrinal, and the members knew little or nothing of the kind of worship Barclay had described. They expected a preplanned service centred in a sermon, and their only Quaker peculiarity was the rejection of the outward sacraments.

In 1872, of course, all this was still in the future. When Elkanah Beard reported to the FFMA on his return from India there were no converts and no church. But the man who was to take his place had already been found. Charles Gayford was the son of a farmer in Essex, baptised in the Church of England, who had left the land and become a grocer in the rural market town of Stansted. He was in rebellion against the formalism of his own church, and in Stansted he began to attend Quaker worshi, and 'found peace' in its inwardness and simplicity. He applied for membership and was accepted in 1870, when he was twenty-five years old. About a year later he volunteered as a missionary, and was in training when Beard returned.

Beard spoke to the FFMA of two matters which were on his mind. One was the need in India for medical service, a need of which he had not only learned from Dr Lazarus, but which he had seen for himself on his travels. He had visited Hoshangabad during his first few weeks in India, and though for himself in 1870 it had seemed right to stay in Benares, he now suggested that Hoshangabad might be considered as a new Quaker base. When Gayford joined Rachel Metcalfe in Jabalpur early in 1873 he found a friendly CMS missionary there, and could understand his difficulties about Quaker attitudes to baptism. They agreed that it would be better for them to work in different areas, and Gayford therefore followed up Beard's earlier investigations of the country round Hoshangabad. The town had formerly been the capital of a small feudatory kingdom of the Mogul Empire, and had been annexed by the British in 1818. It lay on the south bank of the great Narmada river, and on the opposite bank, to the north, was the territory of the state of Bhopal, easily accessible by ferry and (in season) by a pontoon bridge.

Gayford explored the whole region on foot, carrying his camping equipment in a bullock cart. He came very close to the people and saw how great were the medical needs, especially perhaps in Bhopal. Government medical officers assured him that a Quaker doctor would be very welcome, and that Hoshangabad would be a convenient centre from which to work. The FFMA approved the proposal, and all through 1874 Gayford was busy making friends there. He rented an open-fronted shop in the bazaar, stocked it with books, and talked with friendly courtesy to all who came. On market days crowds gathered round, listening to his words with approval: 'Sach bat! bahut achha!' ('That's true! Very good!') they would say. He also made friends with some of the Brahmin boys who attended the Government Middle School, and they came to read the Bible with him – partly no doubt because they wanted to hear English spoken by an Englishman. But the story of Jesus fascinated them as it had fascinated Beard's students in Benares.

There was a widely revered Hindu teacher in the village of Raipur, Pandit Govind Ram, who became Gayford's intimate friend. He brought a mature judgement to bear on Gayford's work. 'We do not differ,' he said. 'Life *should* be lived as Jesus taught, in sincerity of heart.' He urged that the right way forward was not to create a separate Christian 'caste', but to permeate the whole traditional structure, as it stood, with the leaven of the spirit of Christ, and so transform Indian society from within. This was essentially what Keshab was saying, in his appeals to his countrymen to follow the precepts of Jesus without rejecting their own culture; it was what Ranade envisaged when he called for a new sensitiveness to 'the Voice of God in us'. But it was not what Gayford had been taught during his missionary training in London.

During all these months Gayford was spending a good deal of time still in Jabalpur, where Rachel Metcalfe had made friends, as she always did, among the young, especially the young English-speaking 'East Indians'. Among them were some Luso-Indians from Calcutta called Mendes, who belonged to the same Lalbazaar Baptist Church with which some of the Calcutta Friends had been connected. Gayford and Lewis Mendes, an able young lawyer,[2] soon became close friends, and it was not long before Gayford asked Lewis's sister Harriet to marry him. Harriet was a teacher, and Rachel knew her well; she wrote to assure the members of Gayford's Quaker Meeting in Essex that even though Harriet was not a Friend she would nevertheless prove 'an earnest fellow worker in the cause of Christ'.

The time had therefore come to set up a home in Hoshangabad where Rachel and the two young people might live together. Up till then, Gayford had camped in the town wherever he could. A house in the British 'cantonment' area was not possible, for neither Harriet the Luso-Indian nor Rachel the working woman would be accepted as social equals by the wives of the civilian and military officers.[3] If they were to make friends and be happy they must be near *Indian* Hoshangabad, and as no suitable house was available there for rent the natural solution seemed to be to buy land and build, as other missions did. Gayford therefore bought land on the fringe of the Indian town, and in May 1875 he and Harriet were married. During the rainy months which followed they found a temporary home at Sohagpur, thirty miles away, where there was a little 'railway colony' of East Indians. Rachel was unable to help in any way; in the latter part of 1874 she had been seriously ill, and had gone to stay with Bessie Alexander at Agra for what proved to be a very long convalescence. Only in October 1875, when the rains were over, were the Gayfords able to bring her back from Agra to the Sohagpur house.

The young couple were therefore alone when a critical decision had to be taken about the issue of outward 'conversion'. At the end of June 1875 Bal Mukand, one of the boys in Gayford's Hoshangabad Bible class, came to Sohagpur to tell him that he wished to declare himself a Christian. Gayford suggested that this ought to be done at Hoshangabad, before his own family and friends. But by that time the first monsoon floods had made the roads impassable, and Bal Mukand pleaded that there should be no delay. In Sohagpur, at a quiet gathering of the East Indian Christians, he made his declaration, took off the 'sacred thread' of his caste, and cut off his *chutiya*. The action was a renunciation of Brahmin social privilege, a declaration that a disciple of Christ (in John Woolman's words) 'might no longer consider himself a distinct and separate being' from the mass of common humanity.[4] In this at least Bal Mukand kept the faith. There are glimpses of him in later years, sitting with 'untouchable' leather-workers in their homes, and telling jeering Brahmin passers-by, with a good-tempered grin, that 'God and all humanity belong to the same caste'. A very Quakerly remark, though perhaps Bal Mukand did not realise its full implications.

After the floods subsided his father heard what had happened and hurried to Sohagpur. Finding his son in the bazaar he began to pour out reproaches: 'To go and become a Christian without a word to me! And you always such a good obedient boy!' Passers-by stopped to listen, of course, and there was mounting excitement when they realised what the altercation was about. Nevertheless they gave Bal Mukand a hearing; he told them he had acted of his own free will, and both the Brahmin village headman and the schoolmaster stood up for him. 'We know Gayford,' they said. 'His teachings are good. The boy has done nothing wrong.' Gayford himself hoped that when the first shock was over Bal Mukand might be received back into his own home.[5]

The incident, however, brought the latent uneasiness about conversion to the surface. The little school which Harriet had already started in Sohagpur was almost emptied of pupils for a time, for fear that she might turn them into Christians by giving them something to eat which a Christian had touched. After a while she was able to overcome the parents' fears, and the children returned; a few months later, when the monsoon was over and Rachel joined the Gayfords in Sohagpur, she took over the school and carried it on for about a year. When the new house was ready, in October 1876, they all moved to Hoshangabad and the Sohagpur school was closed.[6]

The Gayfords spent a good deal of the cold dry season of 1875–6 living in a tent on their Hoshangabad land and directing the building operations. In Hoshangabad also there had been unfriendly whisperings: why had Gayford been buying land? Why had Bal Mukand's father accepted his son's action so easily? Had he perhaps been bribed? Gayford patiently explained his position and his beliefs, and the more cultured families responded. In April 1876 'two or three hundred respectable Hindus and Muslims' watched quietly while Bal Mukand's school friend Jugal Kishore also declared his Christian faith. During the next twelve months a few others followed suit. There were many more, including Bal Mukand's father, who called thenselves 'Christians at heart', and whose faith, in Bal Mukand's phrase, 'was known in their conduct'.

Although Gayford thus took the first steps towards creating a 'separated' Quaker church, one wonders whether some obscure uneasiness about this policy contributed to his growing conviction that he personally should make a new start. Early in 1877 he asked permission to withdraw from Hoshangabad in order to undergo a full medical training and thus be able personally to meet the need for a doctor. Newman replied that he should not leave until a successor could be sent; Quakers now owned property, and were no longer free, as they had been in Benares and Jubalpur, to come and go as they thought right. It was not until the end of 1878 that replacements arrived.

The year 1877 may be regarded as a turning-point. Up to then the FFMA had made it possible for individual Quakers to make their Quaker witness in India in their own way, with minimum organisation and great flexibility. Once fixed in Hoshangabad it was easier to organise the enterprise as a 'mission' like other Protestant missions. There is no doubt that that was what Newman, Hipsley and their committee wished, and it was probably because they realised that the Beards had a different outlook that they turned down their offer of renewed service. At the same time they accepted with alacrity a young volunteer whom they could regard as one of themselves, Samuel Baker of Dublin, a member of an established Quaker family. His background was familiar, his ability undoubted, and he was active in the Home Mission of Dublin Friends. But he was only twenty-one, and the committee refused to send so young a man to India without 'senior companionship'. Newman found it for him in

1878 in John and Effie Williams. John had previously been an Army printer in India, and was then employed in Newman's printing business; it seems probable that Newman took the initiative and persuaded him and his wife to accept the appointment. They were not Friends; they joined the Society just before starting for India. John was Samuel Baker's senior by fifteen years, but he was not socially his 'equal'; it must have been obvious which of the two men would take the lead.

By this time Rachel Metcalfe was no longer living in the Mission House. During 1876 she had become so crippled that she had to have a wheelchair, and by 1877 she had lost the use of her hands. She would remark with wry humour that she could do nothing now but *talk* – she who had come to India to give 'work not words'! Gayford once called her 'a *cheerful, happy* sufferer', choosing without knowing it exactly the same adjectives which Mrs Leupolt had used of her when she first reached Benares. He had found her somewhere to live 'right *among* the people', where little girls could come to her school more easily. There, in a rented house in the bazaar, she 'mothered' the young converts and seekers whom Gayford had attracted, and helped to find Christian brides for Bal Mukand and Jugal Kishore from Benares and Jabalpur. It was to her that they turned among the changes which now took place.

Samuel Baker set to work with the energy of the proverbial new broom. Gayford's leisurely personal approach was replaced by a planned and strenuous timetable of public propaganda – lectures, sermons, regular open-air meetings in town bazaars, preaching tours in villages. Schools for children were organised, and clinics for the sick, both of which were intended primarily to provide opportunities for proclaiming the Gospel. On the occasion of Queen Victoria's Jubilee in 1887 the citizens of Hoshangabad asked whether Quakers would provide the town with a high school. Baker urged the FFMA to agree, 'in order to give us an influence with the upper classes similar to that which the distribution of medicine gives us with the common people . . . we should use education *only* as a means to christianise'.

This programme demanded buildings and equipment, a paid staff and a hierarchy of power. Quaker missionaries, like so many others, began to 'exercise authority'. Baker, like Russell Jeffrey before him, regarded the British Government as the natural ally of the Christian mission. 'The power of the English government', he wrote, 'commands respect for those representing the Englishman's

religion.' In their second year, Baker and Williams built an impos-
ing 'Meeting House' in Hoshangabad, which was opened in
November 1880 with a fanfare of publicity and with the active
co-operation of British officials. Why? The tiny Indian Quaker
group did not then need it. It seems to have been a kind of status
symbol for 'the Englishman's religion', and Henry Newman, who
visited Hoshangabad a few weeks later, reported that 'it added very
perceptibly to the position of the mission among the people of the
town'. Yet in the same report Newman asserted, on the authority of
a government offical, that 'a number of the *babus* would gladly blow
up our mission house and all of us in it if they dare'. Whether or not
there was any element of truth in the assertion there is a new flavour
in the language used; the contemptuous use of the courteous Indian
title *babu* reflects the British community's dislike and distrust of the
educated Indian. Baker, young and impetuous, was infected by this
more than he realised, though he did know his weakness and strove
to overcome it. His conduct sometimes hurt and alienated those
whom Gayford had attracted; some who had previously been
friendly were now, we are told, 'unwilling' to attend Quaker meetings.

Rachel was troubled by the change of atmosphere. She feared
that the new young converts, who now became part of the staff of
the organised mission, were not getting the personal help they
needed. 'They are very young in the school of Christ', she wrote
tenderly, 'and they need grounding in the love and truth of Jesus –
not long sounding speeches and sermons but sincere *love* in life and
action. It is the *life* that tells – not *saying*: I believe in the Lord Jesus
Christ, but *putting on* Christ.'

This protest, that words and doctrines were taking the place of
'love in life and action', was called out by what Rachel saw going on
in the mission. She was disturbed by what seemed to her to be the
neglect of central Quaker teaching. At the same time Baker's
masterful ways were causing tension among his colleagues; he was
too apt to ignore or override corporate decisions with which he did
not agree. Matters came to a head in 1886. Early that year, while the
Bakers were on leave, the Gayfords returned to Hoshangabad.
They were warmly welcomed, all the more so because eighteen
months earlier they had suffered a loss which touched every Indian
heart – the death of their infant son. Charles, now a qualified doctor,
planned a medical service for Hoshangabad and Bhopal, which had
meanwhile been linked by a new railway line. Hoshangabad was the

obvious base, and the local committee therefore suggested that when the Bakers returned they should live at Seoni Malwa and start the new mission centre for which they had been pleading for three years. The Bakers refused to agree; the Hoshangabad house, they said, was *theirs*, and the FFMA supported them. The Hoshangabad workers resigned in a body as a protest, the medical plan was wrecked, and the tiny Quaker church lost all its educated members. The Gayfords went to Allahabad, where one of Harriet's relatives was a proof-reader in the Government Press, and started a medical service there.

The only useful comment which can now be made about that unhappy dispute – embittered as it undoubtedly was by personal jealousies – is that there were questions of principle involved which, so far as one can see, were never clearly thought out. Was teaching, or the art of medicine, a religious calling in its own right, as Rachel and Gayford believed? Or were clinics and schools merely means to an end, justified only so long as they attracted 'converts'? Was the essential task of the FFMA to 'help those on whom the Lord had laid his hands' to obey their individual calling – as it had helped Rachel twenty years earlier? Or was it to find the staff to run an organised mission? During the period we are discussing the organised mission came first.

By the summer of 1888 the Gayfords were back in England, where Charles practised medicine, for the next twenty years or more, in London. The visit to Hoshangabad in 1886 had disturbed him deeply, not only because of his personal disappointment but because of the difficulties his converts had encountered. The hope that the Quaker mission could avoid the problems of its attitude to baptism by working in a separate geographical area had proved illusory. In contrast to what the FFMA had envisaged, its converts did become 'a narrow sect', they were *not* regarded as 'part of the Christian church', because they were not baptised. Few and vulnerable, they were cut off both from the community of their birth and from religious fellowship with the baptised Christians whom some of them (like Gayford himself) had married. By 1886 a number of them had escaped from unbearable isolation by returning to their original Hindu or Muslim community, while Jugal Kishore had been baptised into his wife's church at Jabalpur. Gayford seems to have concluded that rejection of outward baptism was a mistake, and that his own duty was to labour for the 'permeation' of the church of his birth with the inward 'Truth' which he had found among Quakers.

'After full and careful consideration', he informed his London Quaker Meeting of his decision, and his resignation was accepted with mutual good will.[7]

No record, apparently, remains of Gayford's subsequent medical and religious service in London. He died at Brixton Hill in May 1917, and in those dark days of war the British Medical Association could not publish its customary obituary notices. But Harriet's three-line insertion in the *South London Times* was more than a formality; it paid tribute to the 'loving and devoted husband' with whom she had shared 'forty-two years of most happy married life'. She seems to have been much isolated;[8] little more than three years later her body was buried in her husband's grave.

The Gayfords' withdrawal from Hoshangabad must have been a grief to Rachel Metcalfe, but this time she was not left alone. She had a new and absorbing interest. Five years earlier, in 1881, Bal Mukand's father had brought a little orphan girl and asked Rachel to give her a home. Rachel readily agreed, more orphans followed, in 1883 a house was built for the growing family near the Meeting House, and Ellen Nainby came from England to help. In spite of increasing physical helplessness and pain Rachel was very happy among the children; her vivid affectionate pen-pictures of each little person provide some of the brightest pages in the FFMA reports. In the crisis of 1886 Ellen Nainby resigned with the rest, but later agreed to stay, probably because she could not bear to leave Rachel alone.

When Rachel Metcalfe died in 1889 Friends in Hoshangabad were just beginning to realise how important was her insistence that young people should stand on their own feet instead of 'hanging on to the missions'. A Quaker businessman, Frederick Sessions, who visited Hoshangabad that same year, found only *one* adult in the tiny church who was not in direct mission pay. After studying the situation he found the capital to set up an industrial training unit at Rasulia* near Hoshangabad. He sent one of his own Quaker employees, an experienced builder and carpenter, to manage the unit; even so it might never have got off the ground if it had not attracted the interest of a local mechanical genius, Shiv Dayal. Shiv Dayal had the reputation of being able to tackle anything from blacksmithy to

---

* It seems probable that Rasulia was one of the 'deserted' villages in the Narmada Valley mentioned in *The Land Tax of India* (1830). When Quakers bought land there old men in Hoshangabad told them that in their boyhood it had been 'a large village surrounded by jungle'; in the 1880s it was a tiny hamlet.

watch-making (even, we are told, false teeth), and Friends had the good sense to accept his offer to become their foreman, even though he was 'a heathen'. The new unit's first job was the repair of the town fire-engines, and it soon became 'a veritable hive of industry. If I had needed a brand new *tonga*, a bungalow furnished, or my watch repaired,' wrote a visitor, 'it would have been done creditably.'[9]

With an enlarged missionary staff, bungalows, schools and meeting houses were built not only in Hoshangabad and Sohagpur (where the Williams had started mission work in 1881) but also in Seoni Malwa and Itarsi, and in Sehore, the British Political Agency in Bhopal state. In most of these places some attempt was made to train young people in one or other of the local crafts. A colony of weaver-converts was established at Khera near Itarsi, and both this colony and Rasulia had considerable initial success. The proliferation of railways and government buildings created an abnormally large demand for the furniture and fittings which Rasulia could supply; the widespread famine at the close of the century brought large emergency orders for cloth; but in the end the attempt to make Christians economically independent through traditional crafts ran into the same problem; each craft was the economic preserve of some caste which regarded potential competitors with jealousy. Even at Khera where the Christian weavers possessed the inherited skills of their trade, they depended for the marketing of their cloth upon missionary connections and orders from outside; they were not integrated into the local economy.

A different kind of Christian community came into being among the ancient tribal people who inhabited the forested hills in the southern part of the district. One such tribal group, the Ojhas, had a remarkable chief named Jagaraj. He was attracted by the gospel, and persuaded his clan to become Christian in a body. With Quaker help, they settled in two or three small forest clearings, where they lived as cultivators and herdsmen, and just as this was happening, in 1891, the Quaker mission was joined by George Swan, a man who was specially qualified by his own gifts and experience to understand and help forest people such as these.

George Swan was of gypsy stock, and had spent his boyhood among the companies of strolling players who provided entertainment at English traditional fairs. One evening when he was about fourteen he had gone into a Quaker 'Home Mission' hall to listen to the preaching. Something in what was said spoke to his heart; he experienced a real and lasting religious conversion. He sought out the Quaker speaker, Caroline Pumphrey, and told her that in gratitude to God he too must become a missionary. He could fiddle and sing, but he could neither read nor write. The next seven years held much hard work and hard discipline, but George persisted, became a Quaker, and when he was twenty-one years old was accepted by the FFMA for work in Itarsi, close to the hills and forests.

It is not surprising that George Swan soon felt more at home among the forest tribes than in the conventional society of the mission. He would take his fiddle and concertina and go off for days together, sleeping in jungle hamlets and winning the people's trust by his unselfconscious spontaneity. This was not 'escapism'. He quickly discovered how grave were the injustices to which tribal society was exposed. Unscrupulous moneylenders tempted the simple people into debt, and then used the alien processes of British law to seize their precious lands, in cynical disregard of tribal custom and traditional rights.[10] Swan's fellow missionaries had little interest in such things. For them, the people were 'sinners', 'devil worshippers'. For Swan, they were more sinned against than sinning, and he longed to bring them a Gospel of 'social deliverance as well as spiritual power'. What if they worshipped the sun 'because their fathers did'? They also recognised the 'Great God' who made the sun. Could he not build on that?

This attitude was difficult for most of Swan's fellow Quakers to understand, although Joseph Taylor, who had been living at Seoni Malwa since 1889, shared his interest in the tribal communities. 'Carefully brought up Friends', Swan commented, 'are too innocent by half. They simply don't know what some things mean. How *can* they feel properly for the poor souls who never went through anything the remotest degree like it?' He had been through it; he knew what it was to be hungry, despised, ignorant, bewildered; and, just because he felt so deeply the people's helplessness before injustice, he treated them with what has been beautifully called 'the levity of love': laughed, sang and scolded – and insisted they should take a daily bath!

These forest settlements of Ojhas were, in their modest way, a realisation of Pandit Govind Ram's dream of a natural community living by Christian values. Swan, who had known a close-knit clan life in his own gypsy boyhood, could appreciate the values of the traditional Indian village, bound together by kinship ties and loyal-

ties and by the discipline of natural necessary common work. In his
eyes these were the conditions not only of material prosperity but of
spiritual strength. He warned the FFMA how easily the 'saving' of
isolated individual 'souls' could result in 'a hothouse community of
people called Christians', cut off from the common life and artifici-
ally maintained. He began a serious study of *panchayat* traditions,
and he and Joseph Taylor encouraged each village to manage its
own affairs through its own *panchayat*.

The breath of fresh air which George Swan brought with him died
away before the onset of the calamitous famines of the closing years
of the century. Swan himself died in 1901 at the age of thirty-one,
his powers of resistance weakened by the long strain of a five years'
fight against hunger and disease. The people of the tribal communities were scattered and broken by the calamity; some of them,
in despair, indentured themselves for the tea gardens of Assam.
Mounds of earth half buried in encroaching jungle were all that
remained of the little village clearings where, outside the home-
made mud churches, George Swan had fiddled in the moonlight.

VIII

The Might-Have-Beens 1880–1900

To be at the same time the critic and the friend of government, to help religious insight become political action, remains part of our duty and call.

Clarence E. Pickett, *For More than Bread*

The story of Quaker contacts with India during the critical twenty years preceding 1900 is calculated to evoke in the modern reader a sense of frustration, of missed opportunities. Both among British Quakers and among their Indian fellow seekers there were individuals who might have made a Quaker contribution in the historical process of challenge and response which was then reaching its climax: the challenge to India of the massive impact of Western civilisation and imperialism; the response of the complex forces of Indian life as they accepted or rejected the Western models or were stimulated to develop new forms of political and cultural self-consciousness. Neither challenge nor response was simple or clear-cut; both in Britain and in India there were conflicting currents of thought, and the individual Quakers to whose work we now turn were caught up in these conflicts. Each had some true if partial insight to contribute; our sense of frustration arises from their isolation from one another and from the life of London Yearly Meeting as a whole, so that their partial insights were not pooled and no enlarged corporate vision of what Quaker intercourse with India might mean was achieved.

In the 1880s organised Quaker contacts with India were of two kinds. One was through the FFMA (Friends Foreign Mission Association), which though an autonomous body submitted annual reports to London Yearly Meeting. We have seen in previous chapters how its first missionaries in India, Rachel Metcalfe and

Elkanah Beard, had shared their religious experience in Quaker
fashion by natural human friendships with people of other faiths.
We have also traced the steps by which the FFMA became a
conventional preaching mission with a strongly doctrinal centre.
The change of emphasis from experience to doctrine is vividly
illustrated by surviving descriptions of Charles Gayford in 1874 and
of Samuel Baker about ten years later. Gayford talked of the
experience of Jesus's gift of inward peace, and his hearers understood and responded. For Samuel Baker it was not enough that
people should 'turn to Jesus for peace' unless they would also 'call
him God' – unless they would accept the *doctrine*.

Those whose emphasis was on this exclusive doctrinal Christianity usually had little interest in the problems of poverty and injustice
which had stirred Pease and Bright. George Swan stood almost
alone among the Quaker missionaries of the 1890s in his perception
of the dangers of creating 'a hothouse community of the saved'
while ignoring the exploitation and oppression suffered by the
natural human communities around. The FFMA had no links with
the individual Quakers in India who did interest themselves in these
problems. In 1880 its secretary, Henry Newman, met Martin Wood
in Bombay, but did not treat Wood's work as any part of *Quaker*
concern. Earlier, in 1862–3, Russell Jeffrey's party had travelled to
India in the company of Joseph Pease's son John Beaumont Pease,
but their journal makes no mention of what Pease's business in
India was; it is tantalising to be left in complete ignorance of
whether he was in any way following up those concerns for the sake
of which he had released his father from the burden of family
business twenty-five years earlier.[1]

Apart from the FFMA there were organised Quaker contacts
with India through the traditional Quaker 'testimonies' against the
abuse of drink and drugs, and the Quaker involvement in the
campaign against licensed brothels. There was an active though
unofficial Quaker society for the abolition of 'the regulation of
vice', that is the compulsory medical examination of prostitutes for
the use of soldiers, a practice which was open to serious abuse. In
1886 it was forbidden by law in Britain but still continued in India.
The Quakers Alfred and Helen Dyer were therefore sent to India in
1887, and encouraged to interest themselves also in the opium and
drink problems. The sale of opium to China had been legalised after
China was defeated in the second Opium War of 1857, and there
were opium dens in India too. Licences for drink shops were

auctioned by the government on conditions which made excessive drinking inevitable. A. O. Hume, even before the Mutiny, had bluntly called the drink revenue 'the wages of sin', but his protests had been ignored.

Dyer was a printer by trade. Soon after reaching Bombay he proposed that Friends should take over the weekly *Bombay Guardian*, whose founder-editor, George Bowen, had just died, and so enable him to make it the vehicle of a publicity campaign. The paper had a good reputation; Bowen, a cultured American, had used it to review Indian public affairs 'with comprehensiveness and candour' from a Christian point of view. Henry S. Newman, who had met Bowen during his own visit to Bombay in 1880, welcomed Dyer's proposal; he formed a Quaker Trust and bought the paper.

This might have been a step of great importance. In other hands the *Guardian* might have given Quakers an opportunity to bring their religious and social interests together; it might have been a forum for discussing 'with comprehensiveness and candour' the momentous forces which were shaping India's history during those years. But with Dyer as editor this was not possible. He limited its coverage almost entirely to evangelical religious interests and to attacks on the abuses we have mentioned. Moreover, he refused to print contributions which expressed criticism or dissent, and so stifled real discussion even of the issues with which he was directly concerned. Would-be contributors are said to have complained, probably with justice, that Bowen would have published their comments. There is one appreciative reference to the annual meeting of the Indian National Congress, for its mingling of castes and creeds, and the place it gave to women; but there is no coverage of the major matters which the Congress meetings raised, and much criticism of its association with 'atheists' like Charles Bradlaugh.

Dyer was in touch with the Quaker missionaries, but his obsessive mentality and harsh uncharitable language alienated a good deal of their sympathy.[2] He printed charges of official complicity in unlicensed opium dens in Bombay which he was unable to substantiate in court, and for this he received a prison sentence. Inevitably his credibility suffered, so that his later well-documented exposures of some of the scandals of the drink shops won less support than they deserved. The compulsory medical examination of women was forbidden by a clause added to the Cantonment Act (India) in 1895, but it is doubtful how far Dyer's campaign had any influence on the decision.

In 1893, following a resolution in the House of Commons which declared the opium revenue of the Government of India to be 'morally indefensible', a Royal Commission of Inquiry was appointed. The opium lobby was strong enough to get the China traffic excluded from its terms of reference, which were restricted to 'the production and consumption of opium in India'; but in spite of this limitation the National Opium Committee sent its Quaker secretary, Joseph Gundry Alexander, to watch the proceedings of the Commission in India. He spent about four months in the country in 1893–4, visited the opium-growing areas of Bihar, and was present in Calcutta when evidence was given before the Commission.[3]

Dyer had attacked abuses piecemeal, as isolated wrongs; there is little of the broad sweep of Pease's social concern or Bright's passion for justice. Alexander sought to understand the opium problem in the wider setting of the national life. He concluded that Dyer's charges against Bombay officials, though unsubstantiated, were not wholly unfounded; he saw that no reliance could be placed on the evidence of those who 'took their cue from officials' in order to serve their own interests. He visited the Quaker missionaries in Hoshangabad District, and by the time he reached Bihar he was aware that 'those missionaries who live altogether above the natives' were likely to be ignorant of the realities of the situation, and that the evidence of big landlords who found poppy-growing profitable would inevitably be biased. In Patna he set to work to study the problem from the peasant's point of view, with the help of an Indian pastor named Premchand, who lived among the poor and had first-hand experience of how the opium industry affected them.

There was much evidence, which Alexander considered trustworthy, of the dishonest and oppressive methods by which small farmers, against their will, were 'persuaded' to grow poppy. There was also evidence that men like Premchand, whose depositions on these and other matters might be unfavourable to the government case, were being prevented by various mean subterfuges from appearing before the Commission. When Alexander reached Calcutta he therefore made it his business to ensure so far as he could that such witnesses *were* heard. He was bitterly attacked by a section of the 'Anglo-Indian' press, but Indian newspaper editors sought him out and thanked him for his work, and the Brahmo Samaj assured him of their sympathy with Quaker concerns.

When in due course the findings of the Royal Commission were debated in the British Parliament a Quaker member, John Edward Ellis, took up this aspect of Alexander's independent report. He made an outstanding speech, in which he exposed the unscrupulous tinkering with evidence which cast doubt upon the Commission's conclusions. But progress was very slow; thirty years later the moral issues raised by the opium trade were still unresolved, and J. G. Alexander's son Horace Gundry Alexander paid his first visit to India in 1927 in the same cause.

John Edward Ellis, MP, was the political heir of John Bright, and before the opium inquiry he was already involved in Indian affairs. In 1889, the year of Bright's death, Dadabhai Naoroji and Sir William Wedderburn had organised a British committee of the Indian National Congress, of which William Digby, the former Madras editor, became secretary. John Edward Ellis was one of its two Quaker members; the other was William Martin Wood, who on his return from India had settled with his family in London. From 1882 onwards many Indian visitors were attracted to the Woods' home, for Lydia understood Indian ways, the children had not forgotten their Marathi, and Martin, with his geniality and dry humour, was an excellent host as well as a knowledgeable fellow worker. He combined his interest in India with work for the International Association for Peace and Arbitration, and he wrote a good deal for its magazine, *Concord*. It was uphill work; apathy and ignorance about India were widespread, and Britain's entanglements with Boxers in China and Boers in South Africa raised war-fever to a point where Quakers and other advocates of peace were sometimes in real danger from mob violence.[4] It was not until 1906, the last year of Martin Wood's life, that the political tide in Britain turned, a liberal Government was returned to power, and John Edward Ellis joined John Morley as Under-Secretary of State at the India office.[5] Gopal Krishna Gokhale, who visited England in 1906, must have been one of the last Indian guests to enjoy the Woods' hospitality; Martin died in May 1907. On the memorial stone over his grave is inscribed the Latin verse in which the Roman poet Lucan had paid tribute to Cato: *Victrix causa deis placuit sed victa catoni* – 'With the gods the winning side finds favour but with Cato the defeated'. The words were chosen by Martin's son, Arthur Lidbetter Wood, who knew how true it was of his father that 'his was the politics of a sensitive heart's devotion to the cause of the suffering and oppressed'. There had been over forty years of struggle for apparently defeated causes; Martin Wood had paid no

tribute to the 'gods' of worldly success, but his friends remembered
that he had brought with him, even in the darkest days, 'an atmosphere of serenity and peace'.[6]

Although Martin and Lydia Wood remained Quakers throughout their lives, after their return from Bombay they did not associate
closely with any Quaker group or send their children to the regular
Quaker schools. Perhaps, after the wide range of their interests and
friendships in Bombay they found the mental horizon of many
Friends too limited. This isolation might explain why Martin
Wood's Quaker contemporaries remained unaware of his work in
India, but they seem to have been equally unaware of that of two
men who (unlike Wood) came from well-known Quaker families,
Theodore Beck and Philip Henry Sturge.

Theodore Beck went to India soon after Wood had left, and saw
the country from a very different perspective. To understand his
outlook we must look at some of the developments in India after the
Mutiny and their effect upon two key figures, A. O. Hume and
Beck's mentor, Sayyid Ahmed Khan. Both these men had held
official posts before the Mutiny in what were then called the
North-West Provinces – the immense Gangetic plain which lies
between Delhi and Benares – and they knew and respected one
another. Both had found that the ties of loyalty and affection which
they had established in their districts held firm when the Mutiny
broke out; the Sayyid, who was stationed at Bijnor, was able to save
a number of English lives.

During the next few years, however, the machinery of government was increasingly centralised in the name of 'efficiency'. Hume
found that the local initiatives for local welfare on which human
relationships of trust and good will had been built were now
frowned upon. He and Wedderburn had drawn up a plan for dealing
with rural indebtedness in open village council with the co-
operation of village elders, in the spirit of the traditional *panchayats*. The plan was rejected. The Indian village republics which
Metcalfe had admired were now said to be 'a crude form of socialism, inconsistent with the fundamental principles of our rule'.[7]
Hume was profoundly distressed by the alienation of the government from the people, and resigned from government service in
order to work independently.

The same belief in centralised efficiency led to an increasing
insistence on the use of English in the administration of the country.
Before the Mutiny Company affairs in the Delhi region had been

conducted in the personal style and Persian-Urdu language of the old court, and Sayyid Ahmed Khan had entered its service in 1839 under the old conditions. He was a Muslim of the highest rank – the title Sayyid denotes a descendant of the Prophet – whose family had held distinguished positions in the service of the Mogul emperors. For him the Mutiny had been a specially tragic experience. His own city of Delhi had suffered the full fury of British reprisals; for almost a generation it lay desolate, its cultural and intellectual life blotted out. Such tragedy, he felt, must not be repeated; like Hume he pleaded that it was the duty of a government to cultivate the trust and friendship of its people. The British, he said, should realise how their own attitudes had wounded the Indian spirit, and fomented the discontent that underlay the outbreak: the missionary bazaar preaching, which offended India's sense of propriety by 'blackening other faiths in public'; the alien Western attitude to land ownership and the sense of insecurity it aroused; above all the contempt shown to Indians – 'contempt is an ineradicable wrong'.

It also became clear to the Sayyid that, unless he could induce his own aristocratic community to learn the language and standards of the British rulers, it would be unable to play any part in building a better future. He himself was in many ways a Muslim counterpart of Rammohan Roy, a rationalist reformer with no use for fanaticism or obscurantism. He described himself as 'a cosmopolitan Mahommedan of India'. There were a few others like him, such as Justice Amir Ali of Calcutta and Mahommed Ali Rogay of Bombay,[8] but many Muslims were sunk in inertia, or were prone to regard the study of English as 'little less than embracing Christianity'. Ahmed Khan therefore threw himself into the task which was to occupy the rest of his life, that of providing an education which would enable his community to take an honourable place in the life of the country. The Mahommedan Anglo-Oriental College at Aligarh came into being in 1875–7, with the support both of forward-looking Muslims and of the Hindu Rajputs and others who shared the Mogul-Persian culture.

The Lieutenant-Governor of the North-West Provinces at the time was Sir John Strachey. He knew the Sayyid as a former colleague[9] and helped him to get land and government aid. The Government in fact seems to have been ready to welcome the college for reasons of its own. The Viceroy, Lord Lytton, had written bluntly to the Secretary of State in London in 1877 that the way to 'hold India securely' was not to trouble about 'good' government and popular welfare, but to 'secure and utilise the Indian aristocracy'. A college designed to cater to the aristocracy, established by a man who was prepared to be friendly, seemed to deserve their support.

Sayyid Ahmed Khan had visited England in 1869 when his son Sayyid Mahmud entered King's College, Cambridge, with a scholarship from Benares. In 1883, seeking a new principal for Aligarh, his thoughts turned to Cambridge again. The secular government colleges of India seemed to him to 'leave the inner spirit dead'. He wanted a man who could awaken the inner spirit, and he sent Mahmud back to Cambridge to look for one. Mahmud returned with a 24-year-old Quaker, Theodore Beck, of Trinity College.

Theodore Beck had revelled in the experience of Cambridge, where great scholars and teachers, Henry Sidgwick outstanding among them, drew their students into a lively interchange of thought. Frederick Denison Maurice had been one of the pioneers of this tradition; he was no longer living, but the 'Apostles', the famous society of which he had been the central figure, was still active. The apostolic spirit, said Sidgwick, meant 'the pursuit of truth with absolute devotion by a group of intimate friends, each of whom tries to learn from the other and see what he sees'. New members were chosen with care; the quality of Beck's mind was such that he was invited to join. Among other student members were Sir John Strachey's son Arthur and Kenneth Stephen, whose father, FitzJames Stephen, was the ideologue of the new 'imperial' ideal. These two became Beck's close friends. Naturally, when Mahmud came to Cambridge they introduced him, and Beck, full of generous enthusiasm, was attracted by the idea of helping to create an Indian counterpart of a Cambridge college.

In the summer of 1883 there must have been much talk of India in Cambridge. The historian J. R. Seeley, Maurice's friend and spiritual successor, had just published his book *The Expansion of England*. It treated the British Empire as 'a family of nations', something to be welcomed as a step forward in the organic growth of a human world community. This concept of empire as a partnership of *equals* was the ideal shared by Rammohan Roy and Dwarkanath Tagore fifty years earlier. Seeley recognised that in his own day India did not participate in empire as an equal, and that there had been not organic growth but disruption, 'good and bad destroyed together'. Strachey and Stephen on the other hand were convinced that the imperial connection was for India's benefit; they regarded it as England's duty to 'take up the white man's burden' and *rule*. There could be no question of sharing real power.

The ship on which Beck travelled to India with Mahmud showed him the seamy side of this assumption of the right to rule. It was full of 'Anglo-Indians' who were furious about the Ilbert Bill.* Their racial arrogance disgusted him, and made him all the more ready to listen (in 'apostolic' fashion) to Mahmud's account of the shameful way in which 'the Muslims', the heirs of the glories of the Mogul past, were being subjected to the rule of 'down-trodden Hindu Bengalis' who had accepted government education, whereas they themselves had been too proud to do so. The threat to the ascendancy of the old ruling aristocracy of the North-West Provinces was in fact real enough; they resented the increasing control of the administration by English-knowing Bengalis whom they regarded as 'upstart nobodies', and their own rejection of government education was partly due to their dislike of mingling with their social inferiors in its schools. But this aristocracy was by no means exclusively Muslim, and its dislike of 'Hindu Bengalis' was actuated by regional and class jealousies rather than by religious difference.

Beck soon discovered that the Aligarh college practised no religious discrimination, and that its Hindu and Muslim students lived on terms of friendly equality. He made friends with them all: 'the world for me would be the poorer', he wrote, 'if some Hindus whom I call my friends were not in it'. He won the students' hearts by treating them as equals (a thing they had not expected from an Englishman), encouraging their enthusiasm for cricket, and challenging them with new and exciting ideas in a style of conversation which reminded them of the witty polished talk of the elders in their own cultured homes. Debates in the College Union were modelled on the Union at Cambridge, and Beck got one or two other young Cambridge men to join the staff.[10] The students grew in confidence and self-respect; they organised on their own initiative the club called 'The Duty', which undertook to raise money to enable poor students to attend the college, and sometimes did so by activities (such as running a canteen at conferences) which would earlier have been delegated to 'social inferiors'. During the sixteen years of Beck's leadership there grew up an 'Aligarh image'; an Aligarh man was reliable and practical, and ready to put the wider public interest

---

* The Ilbert Bill was designed to end the anomaly which prevented an Indian member of the Indian Civil Service as District Judge, from hearing criminal suits involving an Englishman.

before narrower family claims or regional prejudices.

Beck's first years in India, however, saw the tragic rift between Sayyid Ahmed Khan and A. O. Hume, old friends as they were, over the way in which the Indian National Congress developed. The two men had much in common; both had grim experience of the Mutiny, and both were concerned that sources of discontent and friction should be exposed and dealt with so that no such outburst should occur again. The Sayyid welcomed united, India-wide action for social service, especially in controlling the religious animosities which 'revivalist' movements, both Hindu and Muslim, were beginning to stir up.* 'His heart', as Dadabhai Naoroji said, 'was in the welfare of India as one nation.'[11] But Hume addressed his first public appeal not to India as a whole but to the graduates of Calcutta University, with the inevitable result that the Congress was dominated by Western-educated Bengalis. Moreover, it was just then that the British residents of Calcutta were conducting the lawless agitation which forced the Government to withdraw the Ilbert Bill. The lesson was not lost on the leaders of the new Congress, some of whom were understandably bitter about the discrimination against Indians in administrative practice. They therefore concentrated not on the social programme which Hume had first envisaged, but on political agitation for the election of Indian representatives to the Provincial Councils. This was a policy with which the Sayyid could not agree; in his view the method of electing representatives by majority vote would not work out fairly 'so long as the people's judgement of the common welfare is clouded by feelings of race, creed and caste'. Nor could he agree with political agitation which 'fomented discontent'. 'I hope', he commented with regard to the Ilbert Bill, 'that my countrymen will not emulate the example of those who think vehement public demonstrations the best way of submitting arguments.' He had already refused to join the National Mahommmedan Association started by Amir Ali because it was too 'political'; for similar reasons he decided not to join the Congress, and concentrated on education, founding and developing a Muslim Educational Conference.

These things are recalled here because the emotions roused by the claim, half a century later, that Indian Muslims were a separate 'nation', and must therefore have a separate State, have made both

---

* He pointed out that the Arya Samaj campaign against 'cow-slaughter', which had started in 1875, had only resulted in *increasing* the number of cows sacrificed by Muslims. It would have been much better to appeal to the Muslims in a friendly spirit,

Sayyid Ahmed Khan and Theodore Beck controversial figures. In particular Beck has been accused of turning the Sayyid against the Congress and being the tool of a British policy of 'divide and rule'. The quotations above are from speeches made by the Sayyid in the Viceroy's Council early in 1883, and show that he had reached the main convictions which separated him from the Congress before Beck came on the scene at all. Unfortunately by the end of 1887 the Sayyid had been provoked into a less dignified outburst by what seemed to him disingenuous claims that the Muslim members of Congress genuinely represented all-India Muslim opinion. There was some painful name-calling on both sides, *any* criticism of government being labelled 'Bengali-style sedition' by the one, and *any* criticism of Congress being attributed to 'fossils and time-servers' by the other.

The records of Beck's part in all this are too meagre for certain judgement. He certainly regarded himself as the Sayyid's 'humble disciple in matters political', and his writings, which reproduce the Sayyid's arguments in detail, confirm his claim. But some of his actions raise puzzling questions. How did the ex-President of the politically conscious Cambridge Union bring himself to forbid the Aligarh Union to debate topical political themes? How did Beck, Quaker and 'Apostle', come to ban pro-Congress newspapers from the College reading-room – a ban which, as he ought to have known, only made the 'forbidden fruit' more attractive to students whose 'inner spirit' he had helped to awaken? All witnesses agree that Beck had an impulsively outgoing nature, and it is clear that loyalty ranked high in his moral code. (In almost his only surviving reference to his Quaker tradition he spoke of the *loyalty* of Friends to Jesus's teaching about oaths.) He had been known in Cambridge as an actor – a gift which carries with it the power of self-identification with another. He seems to have identified himself with Sayyid Ahmed Khan and his work, and his loyalty and affection were increased by the various stormy college crises in which the Sayyid stood by his principal. Many Muslims were still suspicious of a college conducted by a man so 'unorthodox' as the Sayyid, and their fears were not allayed by 'foreign teachers' who introduced such 'Christian' influences as tables and chairs, and knives and forks, into the students' dining-room!

---

as fellow citizens. At the same time he told the Muslims bluntly that it was 'cantankerous folly' to kill cows simply to annoy the Hindus.

In 1895 a more serious crisis arose. Ahmed Khan, now an old man, made the heart-breaking discovery that a trusted employee had been guilty of large-scale embezzlement of the college funds. Public confidence was shaken; widespread famine added to the difficulties; when the founder died in March 1898 the enrolment in the college had fallen to less than one-third and its very existence was in jeopardy. It was Beck's enthusiasm that saved it. With the single-minded devotion to public duty with which he had inspired his students, he organised an all-out campaign to raise a worthy memorial to Sayyid Ahmed Khan by transforming the college into a Muslim university. At a great meeting of the Muslim Educational Conference at Lahore two other men who commanded the respect of the community, Amir Ali of Calcutta and Badruddin Tyabji of Bombay, generously backed the scheme. The Aligarh Muslim University did not formally come into existence till 1920, but the college was saved. The strain of the compaign, however, added to the heavy burdens of the previous three years, had overtaxed Beck's strength; in the summer of 1899, in his fortieth year, he died in Simla.

The Beck family was active in Quaker circles; Theodore's second cousin, Susannah, had planned to become a medical missionary for the FFMA in India, but died just as she was completing her studies. Theodore himself was associated at Cambridge with the Quaker students, led by John William Graham, who could no longer accept the evangelical doctrine of the FFMA, and were trying to restate their faith (as Sayyid Ahmed Khan was trying to restate the Islamic faith) in a way which could meet the challenge of historical and scientific knowledge. For dogmatic 'certainties' he had little sympathy. 'When he wants to abuse a thing', wrote a friend, 'he always calls it doctrinaire.' But he lent one of his Aligarh students *The Imitation of Christ*, and though he spoke little of religion he had an inward strength to which others turned for refuge. When his sister Elizabeth came to India to be married he arranged for the wedding to be conducted in Quaker fashion, as nearly as that could be managed, in his home in Aligarh among his Indian friends. It was clearly a moving occasion.[12]

Reference was made earlier to the way in which Beck's understanding of India complemented that of Martin Wood. They were both, in Beck's phrase, 'unofficial Englishmen' who '*preferred* living in India to living in Anglo-India' and made their friends in Indian society.

Beck condemned the 'supercilious contempt' which too many English people showed towards Indians, and 'the invidious distinctions between English and native officials in the same posts' in the same way that Wood had done. But the India he knew was very different from Wood's. Wood lived in a commercial coastal city, which had not known the terrors of the Mutiny, and did not understand the deep fears that such passions might be roused again. The outlook of his Indian friends was coloured by the 'philosophical radicalism' which had so largely shaped his own youth. Herbert Spencer exercised a powerful influence on Western-educated Indians in the last quarter of the nineteenth century, and Spencer's rational individualism, his confidence in the virtues of reasoned discussion and the ballot-box, is reflected both in Wood's journalism and in the political thinking of the Indian National Congress.

Beck was right to declare that these coastal cities were not the whole of India. He knew the heartlands of the old Mogul Empire, the hereditary chiefs, Muslim and Hindu, whose families controlled the life of the Aligarh District, and the small Rajput States of Bundelkhand, where a Cambridge friend, Theodore Morison, was tutor to the boy-Maharajah of Chhatarpur. He knew something of the life of the Hyderabad State, some of whose leading families had close ties with Aligarh. He was aware of the complex interlocking circles of human relationships, and the many natural bonds of common village origin or common occupational interest which might unite members of different religions; above all he saw the bonds forged by 'a common loyalty to a personal ruler and a common reverence for the saints'.

This last was an insight which was shared by the leaders of western India; Ranade, Chandavarkar and Gokhale were seeking to make this 'common reverence for the saints', with its power to break down the barriers of caste and sect, part of the national ethos.* If Beck had not been separated from them by distance and circumstance, he might have shared with them the idea, derived from Maurice as well as from his own Quaker tradition, that these natural bonds did not go well with 'head-counting' and the overriding by a majority of the wishes of smaller groups.

* In 1894 N. G. Chandavarkar recorded in his diary that at Kalyan railway junction he had noticed two humble railway workers, a Muslim and a Maratha, relaxing together under a tree while off duty and singing verses from Kabir and Tukaram. 'We two are devotees and brothers,' they had said. 'But nowadays there is so little devotion, only the quarrels of the sects' (*A Wrestling Soul*, the centenary memorial biography of Chandavarkar, Bombay 1955).

Both Beck and Wood deplored the fact that (in Hume's words) 'John Bull is not easily moved without a clamour'. But while Wood believed in making a clamour, at least on paper, Beck took a different line: 'I believe that a great reform is needed; but if it is to be brought about, it must be by an appeal to the nobler side of the English character, and not by stirring up feelings of resentment.' Beck, however, might have learned from Wood and his friends that the 'great reform' needed was not only in social attitudes, and that some of the economic discontent was by no means so trivial as he sometimes seems to have thought.

Finally, while Wood praised Indian ways for their common sense and simple efficiency on the material plane, Beck drew attention to the spiritual gifts which India had to offer:

> In estimating the value of India to England most people dwell only on the material side. But India might have a much higher value – a moral and intellectual value. The East which has given birth to every religion which dominates mankind has yet, I believe, something to teach the west. In this age of violent industrial competition, of nihilism, of the decay of old faiths, [India can offer] the gentle influence of ideals of life that belong to a simpler and fresher period of the world's existence. England need fear no impoverishment of her intellectual life by her closer union with India.[13]

'The east has something to teach': that was an insight which no Quaker had before expressed with such clarity or set in such opposition to the *violent* (significant word) standards of his own society.

Beck was almost certainly instrumental in bringing another of his Cambridge Quaker contemporaries to India. This was Philip Henry Sturge, whose grandfather had been a cousin of the Great Quaker opponent of slavery and oppression, Joseph Sturge. He was one of J. R. Seeley's students, and had taken a brilliant degree in history in 1886. A year or two later he was appointed as private secretary to a highly placed official of the Hyderabad State, and in 1890 he helped to found the Nizam's College, which he served for twenty-eight years, first as Vice-Principal and then as Principal. He retired to England in 1918, and died suddenly only four years later at the comparatively early age of sixty-two. Tributes to him speak of how 'he threw himself heart and soul into the life of the College', both as a teacher and as an athlete, and of how he was remembered for his staunch integrity. 'Students trusted and respected him; colleagues were happy to work with him; and officials recognised in him a devoted and loyal servant of the State.' He was warmly remembered in Hyderabad when John William Graham visited the city ten years after he had left. Family tradition is of a man who loved and understood the young; his facility in light verse and humorous drawing must have delighted his Hyderabad students as much as it charmed his little nephew in England.

Two years after Sturge began his work in the Nizam's College, Martin Wood's son, Arthur Lidbetter, came 'home' to Bombay as a junior member of the Indian Civil Service, having passed the examination with a brilliant record in Marathi, and soon showed that he was equally at home in Gujarati. In 1897 he was put in charge of famine relief projects in Nasik. Like his father, he had genial ways, and his cheerful courage put heart into the terrified people when cholera threatened his labour camp. Day after day he worked beside them, and ate his midday meal beside them, sitting on a boulder in the bed of the reservoir they were digging – a picture of him that was long remembered.[14]

His next appointment was as forest demarcation officer in the Thana District. The work demanded much touring and camping; Arthur spent long days talking and working with the tribal peoples whose means of livelihood had to be protected and at the same time reconciled with the long-term needs of soil and forest conservation. At the end of such a day he would settle down with his dogs beside his tent and take out some favourite volume of the Greek classics – for he was not only a practical man but a student and a scholar. It was a strenuous, happy life, even more so after his marriage in Allahabad to Agnes Chicheley Plowden (always known as 'Pip'), and the birth in 1909 of their baby daughter.[15] *People* always came first with him, and files a long way second; they often had to be dealt with by midnight oil.

Martin Wood did not find it easy to understand why his son should become a part of that government machinery whose shortcomings he himself had so ruthlessly exposed. The slight estrangement, and the puzzlement of his father's Indian friends in Bombay, was a shadow on Arthur's life for a time. He and his father had given different answers to the old question which confronts all who would 'mend' the world's institutions: attack from without or reform from within? But he felt himself to be 'guided by the same lights' as Martin had been, though he could not always 'follow in the same paths'. He stuck to his Quaker principles; he refused transfer to the more highly paid judicial service, because he would not be responsible for decisions involving capital punishment. In 1910 he was dismayed to be appointed as Collector of the Salt Revenue, a post which most men in his position would have coveted. He obeyed the discipline of the service, he and Pip enjoyed tours in the inspection yacht (which they mischievously named 'Lot's Wife'!), but he made no secret of his opinion of the salt monopoly. At one point the government circulated a proposal that excise officers should take precedence of the *mamlatdars* (officers of the general district administration) according to the salaries they received. Arthur's comment was blunt and radical:

> There is no reason why we should treat the excise as if its success were more important than the general good government of the country. . . . To rank the *mamlatdar* as inferior is false policy, particularly so when the other officer represents *an unessential and unpopular branch of the administration whose very claim to exist is vehemently questioned*. The wrong is accentuated when the distinction is made on the soul-less and irrelevant criterion of salary.

Meanwhile, Arthur Wood hoped that he might be 'one of the leaders of change' in government practice in India. British institutions, he wrote, were *not* necessarily the best for the country. But he did not live to see the changes of which he had dreamed. In February 1911, out on tour alone, he caught a chill which developed into pneumonia, and was brought back to Bombay too late to save his life. He was widely mourned; the letters which reached Pip from many Indians in humble circumstances, as well as from personal friends of both races, bear witness to the affection he had inspired. India had prematurely lost a friend.[16]

The individual Quakers whose experience in India has been summarised in this chapter might, if their various insights could have been shared with one another and with the Quaker fellowship as a whole, have helped the Society of Friends to a much more complete understanding of India than was possible to those who limited their vision to the mission work in Hoshangabad. Joseph Gundry Alexander's care for the exploitation of the poor, the complementary political insights of Martin Wood and of Theodore Beck, Philip Sturge's knowledge of a great Indian-ruled State,

Arthur Wood's day-to-day work as a compassionate, independent-minded government official: taken together, what a spectrum of experience they represent! There was one more element, of which British Quakers were equally unaware – the experience of the Indian Quaker group in Calcutta.

IX

The Triple Stream

Love was the first motion.
John Woolman
No truth worth knowing can ever be taught; it can
only be lived.
C. F. Andrews

The city of Allahabad, so named by the Muslim rulers of India, has
another and more ancient name. It is Prayag, the Confluence; it has
grown up where Ganga and Yamuna, the Ganges and the Jumna,
flow into one another. All rivers in India are holy, being givers of
life, and this place where two great rivers unite has a special sanctity.
Down-stream the two currents, the one clear, the other turbid, can
be seen to keep their separate identity for some distance. They
merge only slowly, and it is said that as they do so a third divine
invisible river mingles her waters with theirs. This is Saraswathi,
river of wisdom, whose presence gives the triple stream its special
power to cleanse and bless.

The coming of Quakers into the life of India may perhaps be seen
in similar imagery. There were two streams, one concerned with the
public affairs and welfare of the Indian people as a whole, the other
with a religious message to the individual heart and conscience.
Both streams derived much of their power from the renewal of
energy which came into British Quakerism from the evangelical
movement. In the first stream were men like Pease and Bright and
Joseph Alexander and their colleagues, men whose very real personal piety expressed itself towards India in a hatred of oppression
and a passion for justice. The FFMA missionaries formed a second
stream; they were concerned to commend their religion not only in
action but in words, and persuade others to adopt it. The compassionate impulse was often strong, but the *general* tendency of the
mission was to 'take people out of the world' rather than to 'excite

their endeavours to mend it'. In India the two currents ran side by side and scarcely touched – until both began to feel the cleansing power of the 'invisible third', the underground current of the original Quaker experience which, as it re-emerged, brought together the publishing of 'Truth' and the practice of service into the unity they had had in the experience of Fox and Penn and Woolman.

This underground current was preserved in the nineteenth century among the so-called 'conservative' Friends. There may have been sometimes too much timidity, or too much blind clinging to tradition, in their withdrawal from public affairs, but they were right to warn the 'progressive' philanthropists and missionaries that outward busy-ness, however benevolent, must not be allowed to drown the voice of the Inward Teacher. In the name of the inwardness of Quaker religious experience they protested against the emphasis on the idea of 'imputed righteousness'; they also affirmed the original Quaker vision of a 'universal saving Light'. 'The religion of Christ did not commence with Jesus; in all ages the everlasting Father has united himself with man and had revealed his Immanuel nature,' wrote a saintly American Quaker, Job Scott, in 1793. '*Putting on Christ* is not imputation but reality,' wrote another, Hannah Barnard, in 1800. 'It is Christ *in you* who is the hope of glory.'[1] Rachel Metcalfe shared this 'conservative' outlook; she used the same phrases, in the same sense, in her protests against the increasingly doctrinal emphasis in the Hoshangabad mission after 1880.

Although the FFMA leaders and the liberal Quaker reformers worked in India in separate fields, they agreed in some of their basic assumptions. Consciously or unconsciously, they all accepted the utilitarian emphasis on the individual; their appeal, whether in worldly or in spiritual affairs, was to enlightened self-interest.[2] Theodore Beck was the first Quaker in India to take a different view of the dynamics of human relationships, and to urge that these should be founded on respect for living human communities and should appeal not to self-interest but to generous good will. His thinking, in fact, had been coloured by a 'romantic' as opposed to a 'utilitarian' philosophy, in other words by the teaching of F. D. Maurice and J. R. Seeley.

Maurice probably did more than anyone outside the Society to enable Quakers to recover their original insights and relate them to their work in India. He had been involved in Quaker interests all his life, had intimate Quaker friends and owed much to the writings of William Penn. He had begun his career as a journalist with J. S.

Buckingham after the latter's return from India; he backed the British India Society, along with J. M. Ludlow, and with Ludlow he pleaded for 'Christian socialism' in place of the individualist *laissez-faire* economics which seemed to him a denial of human brotherhood.[3] He dreaded the doctrinaire, sectarian spirit which divided men by 'idolising their own notions and systems' instead of allowing them to find unity 'in their families, their countries and as men' through the fellowship of the inward Christ-spirit. Nevertheless, he did not belittle the reason. 'True religion', he insisted, 'must satisfy both the reason and the conscience of humanity.'

Maurice's influence on Quakers was first seen clearly in John Stephenson Rowntree's book *Quakerism Past and Present*, to which reference was made in Chapter V. Rowntree declared that one of the main reasons for the decline of the Society was its long-continued 'disparagement of the human intellect'. During the following decades the need for a rethinking of the Quaker faith became more and more urgently felt, especially by the younger generation of Friends who were beginning to attend the universities. A stormy debate between 'science' and 'religion' followed the publication of *The Origin of Species* in 1859, and the questions it raised could not be ignored. In 1884 three Quakers published a small book called *A Reasonable Faith*, in which they pleaded for 'reverent inquiry', declaring that they could not honestly accept the evangelical language in which official Quaker documents had long been couched. They met with considerable sympathy in London Yearly Meeting. The group at Cambridge, led by John William Graham, was thinking on the same lines.

Quakers in America had for fifty years been divided by a series of separations into various groups. In 1887 representatives of ten of the eleven 'orthodox' yearly meetings met at Richmond, Indiana, and drew up a statement of belief known as the Richmond Declaration, in the hope that its acceptance would promote unity. Some British Friends were present and helped to draft this declaration, and in 1888 it was laid before London Yearly Meeting for its approval. Its evangelical outlook was congenial to many British Friends, but like Maurice they believed that 'notions' would divide rather than unite, and they refused to endorse it. The decision marked a critical turning-point; younger Friends, including scientists and scholars like Sylvanus Thompson and J. Rendel Harris, renewed their efforts to restate their religious experience in terms which science and scholarship could accept.

For Maurice, as for Job Scott, the concept 'Christ' was not limited to the historical figure of Jesus. He is the Light in each human heart; and He is also the creative spirit who inspires all that is 'just, lovely and generous' in *all* religious systems. Seeing these religions as a living part of the human heritage, Maurice challenged the almost universal assumptions on which missionary work was based: 'Jesus did *not* say, Go and convert all nations to another religion. He said, Go and *teach*. So long as we think of Christianity as a Western religion which is to drive out Asiatic religions, it is good for us to find lions in our path of proselytism.'[4] But Maurice did want Christians to *teach*; he did want them to share their knowledge of Jesus the man, the beloved historical person, and his message to the world. In 1865 his younger colleague J. R. Seeley published a study of Jesus as a human leader, one able to call out the enthusiastic personal devotion 'which makes men pure, generous and humane'. He called his book *Ecce Homo* (Behold the Man!); it was reprinted again and again and had a great influence both in England and in India.

All these movements of thought contributed to the spiritual renewal of the Society of Friends in Britain, and their influence was felt in America also. Among the younger Friends in Britain the outstanding figure was that of John Wilhelm Rowntree, while his friend Rufus M. Jones gave expression to the new stirrings of life in America. The new spirit combined respect for the findings of scientific and scholarly research with the enthusiastic 'imitation of Christ' to which Seeley had summoned his generation. 'It is not much use enlightening people unless we can enflame them. Truth and Love were meant to advance together,' wrote Rendel Harris to Rufus Jones in 1897.[5] A few years later, in 1903, the Woodbrooke Centre of Quaker studies at Birmingham was founded for this double purpose, to enlighten and to enflame; it was destined to play an important part in revitalising Quaker relations with India.

It was inevitable that the proselytising spirit, and the attitude towards Indian religion, which had characterised most FFMA work in India since 1880 should be challenged. In 1896, at a conference on foreign missions, the Quaker scholar Anne Wakefield Richardson appealed for 'a reverent, honest, and sympathetic study of other faiths'. She was vehemently opposed by a Quaker missionary from India, Joseph Alexander's friend Charles Terrell, who declared that India's religions were wholly 'black'. The chairman, Thomas Hodgkin, felt compelled to intervene. It is the distinctive task of a *Quaker* missionary, he said, 'to read the palimpsest of the human heart'. It was a striking metaphor. A palimpsest is a manuscript in which the original writing has been partially erased and overwritten by other material; with care and discrimination it may still be read.

It was to be some years before this change of spirit made any impact on the FFMA, which continued to recruit its missionaries from the more evangelical families among Quakers. But in 1896, had they only known it, thinkers like Anne Wakefield Richardson and Thomas Hodgkin might have found an echo of their concern in the reflections of the Indian Quakers in Calcutta.

Little is known of the history of the Calcutta Quakers during the thirty years which had elapsed since 1863. Although circumstances had prevented Rachel Metcalfe from meeting them she must have known of their existence, and it is probable that Charles and Harriet Gayford were in personal touch with them. Harriet and her family were members of the Baptist church in Lalbazaar from which some of the Quakers had originated; and it is at least possible, in view of the smallness of the Luso-Indian community, that the de Cruz who was headmaster of the Mission High School in Jabalpur was a kinsman of the Calcutta Quaker Alexander de Cruz. When the Gayfords visited their Mendes relatives in Calcutta one may feel sure that Charles would join the Quaker group for worship.

Apart from the Gayfords, however, the group remained isolated. Henry Stanley Newman's journal of his visit to Calcutta in 1881 makes no reference to them at all, and correspondence with Australia was a tenuous link. What is surprising is not that many of those who had gathered round Edward May in 1862 had drifted away, but that the group should have survived at all. In 1883 the de Cruz and D'Ortez families were still the leaders, and in that year S. Pir Baksh, who had been intimate with Alexander de Cruz for many years, was formally admitted as a member. Possibly he had held back from full membership as long as he was employed by the Baptist Mission, and felt free to declare himself only after his retirement in 1882. It may well have been he, accustomed as he was to dealing with missionaries, who in 1885 got one or two of the younger Quakers to write to the FFMA, but the contact was not maintained.[6]

In 1884 Prabhu Dayal Misra was admitted to membership. He was not a Bengali, he belonged to a Brahmin-Christian family in Upper India and had been brought up in Delhi, where before the Mutiny the small Christian group shared in the easy good will which then prevailed between the two major communities. Of the family's experiences in the Mutiny, when he was a child of ten, we know nothing; it is all too probable that he saw terrible things. A few years later he witnessed another shattering tragedy: at his elder brother's wedding the bridal *pandal*[7] suddenly collapsed, and the bridegroom and a second brother were both killed. The younger lad seems to have been overwhelmed by the shock; he left home, he renounced 'the world', he put on the ochre robe of the sannyasi. What followed is a blank. When he appears in Quaker records his widowed mother had become a Bible-woman in Calcutta and her home was his base. We do not know how he met the Quakers, but clearly their message had answered his inward need.

'You must be content', said Keshab Chandra Sen to Henry Newman when they met in 1881, 'to let Christianity come to us in its own oriental dress. . . . We are seeking Christ as he was in Palestine, going about doing good and giving the water of everlasting life freely.' Prabhu Dayal took the same position, and presented his Quaker message in 'oriental dress'. Each autumn after the rains were over he would leave Calcutta and travel as a sannyasi to his own homelands in Upper India, 'sharing the water of life freely', but leaving no sect behind him.[8] He had some medical knowledge; grateful patients offered gifts which helped to pay an occasional railway fare.

Keshab Chandra Sen was at that time an outstanding figure in the religious life of Calcutta. He had been deeply influenced by Seeley's *Ecce Homo*, and devotion to Christ was the centre of his teaching. Organised Christianity, however, he regarded as disruptive of the nation; he had all Maurice's dislike of sectarian divisiveness. 'My brethren,' he would say, 'do not hate, do not exclude as the sectarians do, but include and absorb all humanity and all truth.'[9]

Keshab was largely responsible for bringing another religious teacher, Sri Ramakrishna Paramahamsa, out of his previous obscurity. Ramakrishna's *bhakti* and his penetrating peasant wisdom had captivated some of the most brilliant young men in Bengal, including the future leader of the Ramakrishna Mission, Swami Vivekananda. Prabhu Dayal was attracted by his fame, and when the ailing saint came to Calcutta during the rainy season of 1886 he sought him out. Sri Ramakrishna's disciples asked how it was that he, a Christian, was wearing the sannyasi's ochre robe. Misra replied that he cherished India's ancient symbols of devotion, and there was a long discussion in which he seems to have won the respect of Vivekananda and the others. Sri Ramakrishna himself brought the interview to a close with one of his homely parables: There is a great well of the water of life, he said, which supplies the needs of all humanity. Hindus draw water at one *ghat* and call it 'jala', Muslims draw at another *ghat* and call it 'pani', Christians at another and call it 'water'.[10] The fact that in the Bengali original of this story 'Christians' are represented as using the English word 'water' shows how completely at that time Christianity was identified with the foreigner. (Even the Quakers, in one of their reports, spoke of sharing their books with 'Christians and natives'!) The great Christian nationalist Kalicharan Banerji had protested strongly against such attitudes. 'Because we are Christians we do not cease to be Hindus,' he wrote. 'We are Hindu Christians, as much Hindu as Christian.'[11] He was using the word Hindu in its cultural sense; he and Christians like him refused to abandon their Indian ways of life and ape the foreigner.

Prabhu Dayal was Hindu in more than dress; he was a *bhakta* whose devotion sometimes passed into ecstasy. In Quaker meetings he would often *sing* his worship – as other Indian Quakers have done since.[12] His spoken utterances seemed 'incoherent' to the British Friends who visited Calcutta later, and it is possible that the tragic experiences of his youth had left him with some degree of emotional instability. However that may be, the Quakers of Calcutta with all their diversity of racial, linguistic and cultural background certainly worked constructively together. In 1887–8 they planned and published a series of Quaker pamphlets. Baksh wrote them in Bengali, and he and Misra translated them into Urdu and Hindi 'for the use of the people of Upper India'; no doubt Misra carried them on his journeys. The little pamphlets must have touched some sore spots, for a Bengali Christian periodical responded with an abusive attack. Baksh's theme was that people may live as disciples of Christ without leaving their native social milieu and without identifying themselves by baptism with a Christian sect. 'Beware', he says (writing out of the experience of a lifetime), 'of being chained with the silver chains of the missions.' Kalicharan Banerji too had felt those silver chains; the Kristo Samaj which he founded was a fellowship for *unpaid* voluntary Christian service and mutual spiritual support.

Baksh thus took the first step, as spokesman for the group, towards an Indian Quakerism. Yet within a year or two it seemed that the group would disintegrate; in 1890 Alexander de Cruz died, and Mariano and Cecilia D'Ortez retired from Calcutta to their family home at Chinsurah; some of the younger ones had already fallen away, and Baksh and Misra were the only recognised Quakers left. They must have wondered what the future was. Almost at once, however, a new recruit joined them whose enthusiasm attracted others.

The new leader was Poornachandra Sarkar, who lived near Baksh's home in Entally. He was then about fifty years old, a civil engineer with a grown-up family, and had retired prematurely from the Public Works Department because (as was said) he had been 'too conscientious' in a matter of contracts. As a child he had been taught to worship Shiva; as a student he had turned to the Brahmo Samaj; in 1865 at the age of twenty-four he solemnly resolved to follow Christ and (having read about baptism in the New Testament) got his Brahmin cook to sprinkle him with water in token of his decision. After a period of 'carelessness' he had a mystical experience – 'an experience of grace', he called it – while he was out on one of his official tours, and this renewed his devotion. When Baksh told him of Quakers he felt he had found his spiritual home. He brought in other like-minded people, including one of his sons; by the end of 1891 the meeting had nine adult members, seven or more attenders, and seven children in a Sunday school.

Meanwhile Joseph Taylor, who had come as a missionary to Seoni Malwa in the Hoshangabad District in 1889, had begun to correspond with the group. He was not content that Quakers should remain a small local sect; he believed that their message should have a wider impact, and he deplored the failure of Friends to make any adequate response to the appeal from Calcutta thirty years earlier. Perhaps it was because of Taylor's letters that Misra paid a brief visit to Hoshangabad in the course of one of his journeys at the end of 1891. It could not have been a pleasant experience for him. Hoshangabad Quakers did not share his belief in presenting Christ in 'oriental dress', nor his respect for Sri Ramakrishna; he reported to the Calcutta group that their fellow Quakers in central India 'denied that Hindu sages and saints might be truly guided by the Spirit of God'.[13]

Early in 1892 Isaac Sharp and Dr John Dixon, who were visiting India on behalf of the FFMA, did spend a number of days in Calcutta and had some long talks with the group.[14] Henry Newman had asked them to find out whether the Calcutta Friends held sound views 'regarding this cardinal doctrine of redemption through the blood of Jesus'. Baksh and his friends were familiar with evangelical ideas and phraseology; evidently they did not argue, but tried to put their own faith positively. The visitors reported that 'they had more to say of the Divine leading than of the blood of Jesus', but they were nevertheless impressed. Poornachandra, wrote Sharp, 'appears to partake of the gentleness of Christ'.

Poornachandra, who was the most fluent of the group in English, was at that time making a renewed attempt to wrestle with the question of Indian Quaker identity. How much he might have gained from contact with a Quaker scholar like Anne Wakefield Richardson! He himself, educated in 'English' schools where Indian culture was ignored, had never even encountered the *Bhagavad Gita* until his Quaker son one day brought home a copy in Bengali translation. Coming to it fresh in his maturity he was deeply moved, and at once attempted to relate its teachings to Quaker insights. But he had to feel his way alone. Joseph Taylor, who visited the group in 1894, was not equipped to give constructive help in such studies, and, because the FFMA was still the only recognised channel of communication between Indian and British Friends, the Calcutta group was cut off from the help they might have received from the renewal of Quakerism in the West. They did what they could, and the results are preserved in the manuscript completed by Poornachandra in 1896.[15]

The 'gentleness' which had so much impressed Isaac Sharp lends a special grace to the pages in which Poornachandra introduces his book. He calls himself a 'Hindu Quaker', 'by race a Hindu and by grace a Quaker', in the same sense as Kalicharan called himself a 'Hindu Christian'; by race, by culture, by social tradition, he is Hindu, and by 'grace', by divine leading, he is Quaker, for he has followed Quaker guides in his desire to be 'a humble follower of Jesus Christ in deed and truth'. He names these guides: Fox, Barclay, Penington, Penn in the seventeenth century, along with a few nineteenth-century writers such as William Forster and Joseph Sturge. But he quotes only when his own experience confirms what they say: 'Whatever is written must be the outcome of my actual experience and not of mere notion.' He believes himself to be writing in obedience to the clear leading of the Holy Spirit.

The book is called *The Universal Spiritual Religion of God on Earth*. The theme is that a pure religion has been revealed to humanity 'in all ages and generations' by the saints and heroes of every land, for 'all good comes only from God'. Poornachandra illustrates his theme mainly from the heroic Indian legends which had kindled his imagination in his childhood, and from the Bible, which he had studied later; as has been indicated, the range of his knowledge was limited, but he was sure of his principles. He was saying in Indian terms what Job Scott had said; he spoke of Christ, in the imagery common in his day, as the *Kalki-avatara*, the destined Incarnate One of our own dark age.

Isaac Penington's metaphor of the 'shadow' and the 'substance' meant much to Poornachandra. The words are familiar to Quakers:

All truth is a shadow except the last, except the utmost, yet every Truth is true in its kind. It is substance in its own place, though it be but a shadow in another place; and the shadow is a true shadow, as the substance is a true Substance.

The 'great apostasy', says Poornachandra, is to rest content with some partial, 'shadow' truth when there is, in Keshab's words, 'a deeper truth on beyond it'.[16] He regarded all the world's saints as 'true members of the Gospel church of the Substance', and declares that 'one who knows the new birth, and the *substance* and spirituality of the religion of Jesus Christ, has no need to abandon his nationality and his society'. Quakers, he believes, are called to be one of the channels by which the experience of the new birth may come to India – not by calling individuals out of one historical system into another, but by being a regenerative power within all the systems, revealing the 'intenser substance' of which the systems are shadows.

Poornachandra was concerned also with the influence of the 'substance' of the inward life upon personal and social conduct. He would have agreed with John Stephenson Rowntree, who wrote in 1897 that 'the task of Friends is to keep before the nation a Christianity at once spiritual, ethical, and practical in influencing conduct'. These practical ethical aspects were worked out in the second volume of his manuscript, which has not been preserved. The surviving summary of its contents shows that Indian ethical insights and social patterns were discussed in relation to the Quaker social testimonies. Fragmentary as the evidence is, it suggests that the Indian Quakers were groping towards a unifying principle akin to that of F. D. Maurice and of William Penn before him, binding together religious enthusiasm and social concern. Isaac Sharp

commented on Poornachandra's enthusiasm for the Quaker peace
testimony, especially in its 'social and national' aspect. Did he and
Pir Baksh, worshipping and working together as they did, feel the
political tensions in Calcutta which were beginning to draw their
ancestral communities into separate hostile camps?

So the story ends. From 1896 onwards the demands of famine
relief in Hoshangabad absorbed the energies of British Friends, and
Calcutta was forgotten. By 1909 Poornachandra had abandoned
hope of finding a publisher for his book.[17] He was then nearing his
seventieth year, and we do not know how much longer he lived. In
that same year, unknown to him, a young English scientist called
Frederic Gravely, a sensitive concerned Quaker, joined the staff of
the Calcutta Government Museum. Communications were closed;
there was no one to tell him of the existence of the group. By the
time Joseph Taylor came to live in Calcutta in 1919, Poornachandra
was gone, and without his leadership the Meeting had finally broken
up.

X

Cross Currents

What we think of as ordinary philanthropy is not
enough. It does not touch the poverty of the soul . . .
we fail those whom we have made our friends just
where their need is greatest.

George Hare Leonard, *Nobler Cares*

The famine of 1896–7, during which Arthur Lidbetter Wood had
worked in Nasik, affected a very large area of north and central
India, including the Hoshangabad District and the stretch of country to the north of it which was under the rule of Indian princes –
Bhopal, Gwalior and the small Rajput States of Bundelkhand. In
1896, just as the famine was beginning, an American Friends mission was established at Nowgong, the British cantonment town in
the Bundelkhand area. For the first time, therefore, Quakers from
both countries were actually on the spot when the emergency took
place. It was a long struggle, for after a better season in 1898–9
there was a second period of dearth in 1900. In Hoshangabad
Quakers co-operated with government officials in carrying out the
provisions of the Famine Code, setting up refuges for the destitute
and public relief projects for the more or less able-bodied. In
Bundelkhand, where the Famine Code was not in operation, they
did whatever they could in a more personal way.

Individual Friends in Philadelphia and New York had been taking an interest in the Hoshangabad mission and helping to support
Rachel Metcalfe's orphans. The mission in Nowgong, however, was
sponsored by a different group, Ohio (Damascus) Yearly Meeting,
many of whose members had been gathered as the result of a recent
religious 'revival'. Such 'revivalist' Friends often knew little of the
experience of historical Quakerism, and Ohio had repudiated the
'so-called doctrine of the Inward Light' as being 'dangerous,

unsound and unscriptural'.[1] In 1892 two women from this Yearly Meeting, Esther E. Baird and Delia A. Fistler, volunteered to become missionaries in India; after three years of language study and general experience in the American Methodist Episcopal Mission at Lucknow they decided, on the advice of a British army chaplain, to begin their work at Nowgong, in the midst of the small Rajput States.

Up till the time of their arrival Esther and Delia had not realised how serious the food situation had become. Without warning, they found themselves surrounded by desperate, famine-stricken people. They were disappointed that the 'preaching of the Gospel' had to be postponed, but they did a fine job. After a quick survey of the area, they got grain from the British Army (at first on credit) and took weekly supplies to specified village centres by ox-cart or elephant. The destitute who flocked to them were passed on whenever possible to the Quaker refuges in Hoshangabad, but there were about fifty children whose parents begged for them to be kept in Nowgong until they could come back to claim them. Only three survived to do so, and the Americans persuaded two motherly Indian women whom they had known in Lucknow to come and make a home for the orphans; it was an affectionate, happy home, and the children grew up to be the nucleus of the future Quaker church.

Esther and Delia described some of their experiences in their letters home appealing for help.[2] A widowed mother in one of the villages they visited won their generous admiration for her uncomplaining dignity; she kept her five hungry children scrupulously clean in spite of all their privations, and thanks to the Americans their lives were saved.[3] One day a crippled boy had dragged himself into Nowgong exhausted by hunger. Little by little he was able to tell his story. His name was Hiralal, and he came from a village many miles away. Crippled as he was, he had felt himself to be a 'useless' burden on his family, so he had crept away from home in order that his share of the scanty food might go to the 'useful' ones. Somehow he had made his way through the jungle and lived to reach Nowgong. One wonders how Esther and Delia reconciled this unselfish heroism, which greatly moved them, with the idea that 'the so-called Inward Light' is an illusion.

The onset of famine seems to have taken the Hoshangabad Quakers almost by surprise; even in 1896 their reports contain only a casual reference to 'the destitution around us'. Many of them had little interest in the economic causes of the disaster, and when famine came they called it 'an act of God'. 'May not God be sending this distress', wrote one of them, 'to arouse people from their sins and draw them to the Lord Jesus?' That seems a strange question now; it was a strange question to many Quakers then.[4] But the missionaries asked it in all sincerity, and they spent themselves both in organising relief and in proclaiming their religious message to those who came for help. As an established mission with the confidence of the officials they were able to work on a much larger scale than the two brave lonely women in Nowgong; the Khera weavers worked to capacity to meet the demand for cloth, and the Rasulia works made tools and water-carts for large government and mission relief projects.[5] When the famine was over there were about seven hundred destitute children in the Quakers' refuges and orphanages, and they took charge of nearly three hundred more from the government refuge at Hoshangabad who had remained unclaimed by any kinsfolk. Orphanages, in their view, were an opportunity for 'lifting children out of the horrors of heathenism' and bringing them up as Christians.

This policy was a matter of controversy both in India and among Quakers. As long ago as 1824 Rammohan Roy had pleaded that famine relief should be carried out in a way which respected religious taboos and traditions; Sayyid Ahmed Khan had pointed out that the arrangements made in 1838 to bring up famine orphans as Christians had contributed to the popular fear that government was interfering with religion. During the Deccan famine of 1877 William Digby had praised the Nizam's Government in Hyderabad for its care in this matter. No one, these men declared, should be asked to sacrifice self-respect, by breaking rules held to be sacred, in order to satisfy hunger. The Hoshangabad Quakers, like most missionaries, took an opposite view. 'One rejoices exceedingly', they reported, 'that *by hunger or any means* the seemingly impregnable fortress of caste is being broken down for the Gospel message to find an entrance.'[6] That was natural enough, given their belief that men and women were 'eternally lost' unless they became Christians. By 1896, however, an increasing number of their fellow Quakers were rejecting these notions. Why, they asked, should children saved from famine not be brought up in their ancestral faith?

In the middle of the emergency such questions were not as simple as they may sound. A baby clinging to its dead mother by the roadside called out an immediate compassionate response, and in the circumstances, amid such urgent human need, it may well have been almost or quite impossible to make any provision for caste scruples. Nevertheless there is no evidence that the missionaries had any wish to do so, and the consequences might be tragic. Kind, motherly Katherine Taylor was haunted for the rest of her life by some of the scenes she had witnessed at the refuge at Seoni Malwa. Parents had come seeking their lost children, and recognised them, and then turned away, accepting the agony of renewed separation because the children's caste had been destroyed. To Katherine, the caste rules seemed narrow and inhuman; from another point of view the missionaries' creed might seem equally so.[7]

During the famine years the Quaker missionaries were in touch with a fellow worker whose approach to these problems was very different. This was Pandita Ramabai Medhavi, who as a Brahmin girl of seventeen had been through the terrible Deccan famine. Her parents had died of privation, but she had survived, and soon won recognition as a pandita – for her father, defying custom, had educated his daughter in Sanskrit learning. After her young husband's death she devoted herself to women's education, went to England in order to perfect her knowledge of English, and after a visit to the United States returned to India determined to help Hindu child widows to become educated and useful members of society. Quaker women in America helped to raise money for her plans, and her Widows' Home was opened in 1887. Rachel Metcalfe was still living; if she heard of it, how she must have rejoiced!

Ramabai's religious experience had led her, after mature reflection, to become a Christian, but her homes were neutral ground where all were encouraged to keep their own religious law. She knew the depth and purity of the faith that had sustained her own saintly father; she could not regard Indian religions as wholly evil nor the people who lived by them as 'eternally lost'. She visited Bundelkhand and Hoshangabad more than once during the famine, and did much to lighten the burden on the Quakers by taking charge of child widows, deserted women and others in special need. She was one of those 'Hindu Christians' who treasured their ancestral heritage, and whose position closely resembled that of the 'Hindu Quakers' in Calcutta. In her life a religious witness, open but humble, was united with untiring service of the needy and with a clear-eyed concern for public affairs. She supported G. K. Gokhale, for example, when he stood for truth against popular clamour and prejudice.[8]

The various Quaker groups and individuals in India, isolated as they were from one another and working in ignorance of one another's concerns, could not yet make any such unified witness. Quakers in Britain too were divided by the impact of the 'new' thinking, and the mission in Hoshangabad attracted mainly those who continued to feel at home in the evangelical tradition. The religious education of the hundreds of orphans, who in a few years' time formed three-fourths of the total membership of the Quaker church, followed the old lines. Worship in the meetings at Hoshangabad or Sohagpur, reported a visitor, was 'something like a mission meeting in England', with set hymns, readings and sermon. Attempts at 'unprogrammed' worship were not successful; a spontaneous 'spirit-given' ministry was so rare as to call for special comment. Moreover, the years which followed the famines were a period of great difficulty. Many workers were physically exhausted and several died. There was inevitably much sickness among the orphan children, and a succession of outbreaks of plague disrupted the whole community. It is not surprising that there was discouragement. The sensitive Joseph Taylor wrote sadly, after nearly twenty years of apparently unrewarded work, that the mission seemed to have reached 'middle age, when there are weeds in the heart'.

'Middle age' tends to be timid, to shrink from new challenges; there are signs of a 'ghetto mentality' in the anxiety that Christian families should live apart from the general population in order to be saved from 'contamination'. In the schools too the 'Christian' atmosphere had to be maintained, even if this meant dismissing efficient reliable Hindu teachers in a way that must often have seemed unjust, in order to appoint Christians.[9] Even co-operation with other Christians was not whole-hearted; Quakers did support the India Sunday School Union,[10] but they hesitated to send boys even to a Christian college unless they could live in a hostel with 'one of *our own* missionaries'! They shrank too from the challenge of the widespread national awakening which began in 1905. At that time their relationships with the government were exceptionally close. The Rasulia Industrial Works, which had failed to attract any significant number of Indian customers, were largely dependent on orders from government undertakings – the Public Works Department, the Post Office, the railways. Useful Rasulia inventions, such as an improved plough and a hand-operated winnower, were publicised through the officers of the Agricultural Department.[11] On the other hand, the positive forces of the national movement were not yet much in evidence in the area. The missionaries were more conscious of the influence of B. G. Tailak's anti-British propaganda, shown in the recurrent rumours that 'the British' were spreading plague in order to reduce the Hindu population. The result was that many missionaries were eager 'to uphold the cause of loyalty'; their attitude encouraged the idea that Christians *ought* to support the government, and made it easy for hostile critics to call them government stooges.[12]

The growing national consciousness was not the only factor that was transforming the life of India. The 'drift to the cities' was beginning, and the young Christians of Hoshangabad, who had so little place in the traditional economic structure, were among the first to be affected. Itarsi, with its major railway junction and its timber trade, was growing by leaps and bounds, and government officals, conscious of the changing situation, urged that any future Quaker hospital or high school should be located at Itarsi as the older towns, Hoshangabad and Sohagpur, already had some government provision for medical and educational needs. The Quakers were reluctant; their first short-lived hospital was at Hoshangabad, their second plan was for Sohagpur, and it was only when their hopes for a site there failed to materialise that in 1914 they finally accepted the government land at Itarsi. The story of the high school was somewhat different, but that too was finally developed at Itarsi, though not till years later.

India was also finding new moral leadership. In 1905 G. K. Gokhale founded the Servants of India Society, the spiritual successor of Ranade's *Prarthana Samaj*, and attracted some of the best and ablest men in the country to sacrificial national service. Rabindranath Tagore was embodying an Indian vision of education in his new school at Santiniketan, and publishing essays on India's political and social problems which challenged accepted ideas and stimulated thought. In South Africa, M. K. Gandhi was learning and teaching the revolutionary method of peaceful *satyagraha* in the cause of justice, and writing his revolutionary little book *Hind Swaraj*; thanks to Gokhale and others, he was becoming more and more widely known in India. Everywhere there were men and women who were exemplifying Penn's maxim that 'true godliness don't turn men out of the world but excites their endeavours to mend it'. It was no longer enough for Quakers to muddle along in their old established routine. Some basic rethinking of their relationships with India was overdue.

The man who exercised the most profound influence upon this rethinking was C. F. Andrews. He and Arthur Wood had gone up to Cambridge at the same time, in October 1890, and though they were not in the same college it is possible that they knew one another, for they both read classics and they both were rowing men. Wood the Quaker died young and unknown; when he died Andrews was still in the first phase of his remarkable Indian career, and his name was already widely known both in India and in England.

In Cambridge, Andrews had wrestled with the same intellectual and moral difficulties as the young Quakers of his generation, and found the clue to 'a reasonable faith', as they had done, in the thought of Maurice and Seeley. His immediate guide was Brooke Foss Westcott, Bishop of Durham, a distinguished scholar, an outspoken champion of the right of the coal-miners of his diocese to more humane working conditions, and one who supported Martin Wood and *Concord* in the unpopular campaign for international justice. Like Maurice he saw the working of the One Spirit of God in 'whatever is just, lovely and generous' in the religions of India. 'Have we the faith', he asked, 'to say of India as Augustine said of Hellenism, "The very thing which is now called the Christian religion existed among the ancients and never failed"?' Westcott was one of these who planned St Stephen's College, Delhi, whose staff Andrews joined in 1904. Sushil K. Rudra, then Vice-Principal, had a passionate love of India, and he and Andrews quickly became intimate friends. The friendship cured Andrews of all sectarian narrowness in religion, and made him in public affairs an ardent champion of the Indian point of view.

The influence of the two friends was soon felt in Britain also. Along with some other thoughtful Indian Christians, G. C. Chatterji, K. T. Paul and S. K. Datta, they began writing articles in British magazines such as *The Student Movement* and *The East and the West*, which made a powerful impact upon young people in all the churches, including young Quakers. They quoted the religious insights of Kabir and Tukaram, of the Sikh *Granth Sahib* and the Buddhist *Dhammapada*. 'That God hid himself from men like these, who sought him with such consuming passion', wrote G. C. Chatterji, 'is a thought that India can never accept.' They asked the universities of the West for 'Christian gurus and Chaitanyas'[13] who would be willing 'not merely to share your lives with us, but to let us share our lives with you'. Many young Christians responded; they came to India not to proselytise but to make friends, 'to stimulate thought, inspire belief, and leave the spirit of Truth to guide men into truth'.[14]

In 1910 Henry T. Hodgkin returned from teaching in China to become the new secretary of the FFMA in London. Life in China had taught him how precious was the variety of human religious experience and of the customs and traditions which embodied it. In 1911 he set in the forefront of his annual report some words of N. G. Chandavarkar, to which Andrews's writings had drawn his attention, about the *permeation* of Indian thought and life by 'the ideas which lie at the heart of the Gospel'. For many years Indian friends of the Quakers, and the Indian Quakers themselves, had been using that imagery of permeation; now, with Hodgkin's encouragement, two new Quaker missionaries, Geoffrey Maw and John Somervell Hoyland, carried this principle into their work in India.

Geoffrey and Mildred Maw were 'enflamed' like Andrews by love of Jesus Christ. Andrews called his autobiography *What I Owe to Christ*; Geoffrey described himself as Christ's 'debtor'. Philanthropy was not enough for either; both knew that 'outward works of benevolence' could only meet men's real need in so far as along with them one could 'pass on the life'.

Geoffrey Maw came of a Quaker banking family and had completed his own training in a bank; in preparation for his work in India he also underwent some elementary medical training, which showed him to be 'a born doctor'. He and Mildred both attended the Quaker Missionary College, Kingsmead, but it was only when they reached India that their eyes were fully opened to 'the beauty of holiness' in the lives of men and women who knew nothing of the historical Jesus. It was Geoffrey's delight to talk of Jesus to all who were willing to listen; if the story 'inspired belief', so that some desired to become disciples, he believed that 'the Spirit of Truth would guide them into truth' and show them what they ought to do. It was not for him to lay down rules.

The message was given in Indian idiom. Geoffrey and his companions Khushilal and Dharmasevak travelled on foot as sadhus with no money in their purse and with their few necessities tied in a cloth and slung over their shoulders. They would camp under a tree on the outskirts of a village and accept whatever hospitality the villagers offered. This, thought Geoffrey, was how Jesus had sent out his first messengers; why should not the same blessings attend them in twentieth-century India as in first-century Palestine?

In twentieth-century India, however, Geoffrey could not avoid being recognised as a member of the ruling race; in the eyes of many his eccentric behaviour could only mean that he was a government spy! Such rumours were a nuisance, but a sense of humour helped. 'If I were really in the Secret Police, as is widely supposed', he wrote, 'I should have excellent opportunities! Finger-prints, for example – there are few better recorders than the shiny surface of a freshly peeled egg, standard hospitality in the area where we are now working.'

But rural India did resemble Palestine in other ways. Much sickness was regarded as demon-possession, and as Khushilal himself came from a family of traditional exorcists he knew the hopes and fears of the people. Geoffrey, the 'born doctor', felt more and more impelled to offer himself as a channel of healing spiritual power. One day the right moment arrived. The party came upon a man who was crouching over a little fire and shivering with fever. With his consent they laid their hands upon him and prayed, and then left him. 'They took my fever away with them', the man reported afterwards to his fellow villagers, 'and it has not come back.'

As in Palestine, the news of the healing spread rapidly, and others came asking for help, often when all other resources had been tried in vain. One evening near-despairing parents called them to see a little boy who lay, to all appearance, very close to death. They prayed long and earnestly with the family, but there was no visible change in the child's condition. Finally, late at night they withdrew to their camping-place, and when morning came they hardly dared to go to the village for fear of what they might find. When they did go the child was playing in the courtyard of his home, well and happy.

Geoffrey regarded these healings as a gift of God such as had been given to many down the centuries. He was grateful, but he did not regard them as of central importance in his work.

Another part of Indian religious idiom was the tradition of pilgrimage. In Hoshangabad District itself there were pilgrimages to the mountain shrine of Mahadeo, the 'great god' of George Swan's aboriginal friends; Geoffrey's generation of Quakers no longer condemned but recognised the 'inward glory' of spiritual meaning in the journey. But the greatest pilgrimages were to the shrines of Badrinath and Kedarnath in the high Himalayas, and on several occasions Geoffrey and Khushilal shared the hardships of the pilgrim route, experiencing its ever-present risks and its spiritual exaltation.[15] In the comradeship of the road and the halting-places there were opportunities for leisurely, deep-going talk with spiritual seekers from all parts of India. There were no 'converts', none were sought, but many lives were touched; among the pilgrim throngs were sensitive souls who perhaps saw in Geoffrey's devotion and humility an embodiment of the great Hindu ideal of *nishkama karma*.[16]

On these occasions Mildred willingly liberated Geoffrey for his special calling, while she and their children stayed in Hoshangabad or some other small town in the district. There both she and Geoffrey brought a reconciling love into the local personal tensions. Horace Alexander, seeing them at work, commented that Friends who like himself were busy with reconciliation between nations were apt to forget that much of the world has not yet learned to live in peace with its next-door neighbour! 'If young Friends', he wrote, 'can build the New Jerusalem in the mushroom town of Itarsi, it may be done even at Geneva!'

Geoffrey had one more gift, a skill in calligraphy which added clarity and dignity even to the mission account books with which his early training had qualified him to deal. Happily this skill found expression also in the transcriptions of great prayers and meditations which he chose and lettered in his leisure hours. One of these, St Paul's Hymn of Love, has looked down Sunday after Sunday on the worshippers in the Quaker Meeting at Delhi. The words have been reflected on and treasured by men and women of many religious traditions, some of whom knew nothing of St Paul and most of whom knew nothing of the man who set his words before them.

Geoffrey's spirit and calling seem to have been not unlike those of Elkanah Beard, Charles Gayford and some of the Indian Quakers in Calcutta. Most Quakers who have followed have been not sadhus but householders, earning a family livelihood or maintained as staff on some Quaker 'project' or 'centre' with local responsibilities. But the Quaker projects and centres of the middle years of the twentieth century all gained immeasurably by the occasional presence of one Quaker sadhu, Gurdial Mallik, of whom more will be said later. He was Geoffrey's successor, though by no means his copy, and he was himself a disciple of Andrews.

Geoffrey's contemporary, 'Jack' Hoyland, also became Andrews's disciple. The Woodbrooke Quaker Study Centre was opened while he was still at school in Birmingham, and while he was at Cambridge his father John William Hoyland became Director of Kingsmead. He was thus from the beginning in touch with the renaissance of Quaker life which had begun in the 1890s. In the summer of 1905, just as he was leaving school for Cambridge, Andrews came back to England for medical advice. His home too was in Birmingham, and Jack was deeply impressed by his talks, which turned his own thoughts to possible future work in Christian education in India. By 1910 the reopening of the Hoshangabad High School was being considered, and Jack, who had by then taken his degree, was provisionally accepted for service there. Meanwhile his magnificent physique, alert mind and Christ-centred spirit made him a natural leader among young Friends on both sides of the Atlantic.

Jack accompanied Andrews back to India after the latter's next visit to England in 1912, and spent much of the next few months with him in Delhi, making friends with Sushil Rudra's son Sudhir, studying Hindustani, and absorbing Andrews's ideas. Andrews taught the two young men, in the spirit of Maurice, to appreciate the strengths of India's traditional human communities, and the danger that an individualistic sectarian religion might be a disruptive force. At a time of bitter hostility between Christian missionaries and those of the Arya Samaj, Andrews took Sudhir and Jack with him on a visit to the Mahatma Munshi Rama at the Arya Samaj Gurukula at Hardwar, and so broke out of the vicious circle of mutual recrimination. He *listened* to the Mahatma, welcomed all the 'Truth' in his position, asked quiet questions, and made friends. 'I remember thinking even then', wrote Jack long afterwards, 'that this [person-to-person friendship, inspired by the 'ethical enthusiasm' of Christ] might be the manner of working which the Spirit of God had chosen for the saving of India.'[17]

The following November, after his marriage, Jack went to Delhi again, and Andrews took him to meet G. K. Gokhale, who had recently returned from a visit to South Africa, and who had the courage to ask crowded meetings of excited students how they could condemn discrimination against Indians in South Africa so long as they practised 'untouchability' at home. Andrews himself was about to start for South Africa to meet Gandhi; Jack took back to Hoshangabad these glimpses of a wider world of national and international life to share with the young people of the little provincial town.

The Friends High School at Hoshangabad had been closed for nearly twelve years, partly because of difficulties of staffing and partly because it could not compete effectively with the Government High School. The government, as was said above, would have preferred the school to be at Itarsi, but agreed in 1913 to the reopening at Hoshangabad. For the next four or five years Jack and his wife Helen devoted themselves, by concentrated attention and 'infectious personal example', to what they believed should be the aim of a Quaker school: 'to permeate Indian society with the values and standards of Jesus'.

Numbers were small, only 113 to start with, so that it was possible for students and staff to know one another as friends. Soon, with Jack to lead them, the boys were eagerly building their own boats and launching them on the Narmada, barriers of race and caste all forgotten in the happy excitement. In class, they were arguing about the national hopes of India, and the programme of the Home Rule movement, in the light of the teaching of Jesus.[18] In the school hostel, Christians, Hindus and Muslims were living on friendly terms as Hindus and Muslims had done at Aligarh. When the terrible epidemic of influenza swept over the district in the closing months of 1918 Jack appealed to them all to help, and himself led the teams of boy volunteers who visited the terrified villagers with medicine, advice and practical assistance. The boys worked magnificently; Jack's own service was recognised by the award of the Kaiser-i-Hind medal. But then came personal tragedy; in January 1919 Helen Hoyland died of enteric fever, and her baby son did not survive her. Jack took the two older boys to England to be cared for, and when he returned to India he did not go back to Hoshangabad. The experiment was over. The High School could not be properly staffed, and after a time it was closed again. When high-school work was resumed, it was in Itarsi and on conventional lines.

Jack Hoyland's attempt to give the Hoshangabad High School a new start was a Quaker response to the widespread criticism of secular government education which had been voiced by Sayyid Ahmed Khan and by many others after him. 'The spirit of selfishness', wrote S. K. Datta about 1908, 'holds Indian education in its grip.' But that grip could not be loosened merely by adding religious observances of some kind to the secular timetable. Penney had observed nearly a century earlier that education was being sought 'as a medium to wealth'; it was an avenue to personal security, and this was increasingly true as it became the general practice to require a certificate of educational attainment from those seeking salaried employment, government or other. The pressure of the demand for certificates tended to force all education into the same conventional mould, and this pressure was particularly felt by the young people who had grown up in the Quaker orphanages. They were socially isolated, and the only jobs readily available for them were of the salaried kind to which conventional education was the passport. Both the Quaker Girls High School in Sohagpur and the boys' in Itarsi were to grow out of well-established 'middle' schools, and to accept the pattern of government-regulated teaching. The local Quaker community did not wish it otherwise, and much faithful work has been done within the pattern. The Sohagpur school, as a largely residential community, has added another dimension; under the leadership of a succession of devoted women, English and Indian, it has given generations of girls an experience of happy corporate life in a way which was hardly possible for the non-residential school in Itarsi. In terms of Indian 'bookish' education, the standards in both schools have been high.

Jack's vision of an Indian *Quaker* education went beyond this, though it was never fully worked out either then or later. The first Quakers, including George Fox, had cared much for their schools, and it is fascinating to see how closely their principles correspond to those which Tagore and Gandhi were advocating for India. Fox desired that children should be brought up in close touch with the wonders of living nature; Penn urged that they should be encouraged in their love of making things, and that their natural energies should be used in 'building houses or ships, but agriculture is especially in my eye'. John Bellers, Penn's younger contemporary, believed strongly in the value of co-operative useful work, and summed up its virtues in words which could well be used of Gandhi's scheme for 'basic national education' in India: "'Tis labour sustains, maintains and upholds; the hand employed brings profit, the reason used in it makes wise, and the will subdued makes them good.' Jack's dreams of community schools for the outcaste leather-workers and basket-makers, in which along with their hereditary crafts they should all practise agriculture, seem to echo these ideas. But the dreams never materialised.

It is easy to see now, with hindsight, that if the hundreds of orphans were to grow into spiritually vigorous men and women, able to sustain the free lay ministry of Quaker worship and the corporate responsibilities of Quaker ways of life, what was needed was what every new Quaker generation needs, a free and fearless education and the opportunity for service.[19] A few of them, for a few years, got a taste of such an education with Jack Hoyland in the Hoshangabad High School, but for the majority the mental horizon was bounded by the timidity of which we have spoken; in addition, the habit of dependence upon a 'mother-and-father' mission engendered by the circumstances of the orphans encouraged an attitude of mind which expected to receive rather than to give, and weakened the impulse to service. Nor were failures of insight and imagination all on one side. In 1910 Francis Kilbey, who as a poor London boy had been stimulated and inspired by a Quaker adult school, was making the Quaker Bible School at Seoni Malwa into a kind of Indian adult school, where young men were introduced to the wonders of nature and of scientific discovery as well as to a deeper understanding of their religion. Not long afterwards the school was closed, because 'modern' Quaker visitors from England feared that it might promote 'a hireling ministry'. In view of the history of the mission the objection seems somewhat imperceptive, but there was at the time no united vision of what kind of Quaker education was needed, either for the nurture of the young Quaker community itself or for the enrichment of the larger Indian society around it. The difficulties were enhanced by the world war. Jack Hoyland's experiment in the High School was carried on almost wholly under war conditions, amid grave problems of communication and of finance.

The development of the Bundelkhand Quaker mission was parallel but somewhat different. It grew very slowly and for many years remained poor; except for the two women who had come from Lucknow it employed no workers from outside, and the most able of the first orphan children became teachers and leaders as they grew up. In course of time the same problems arose as in Hoshangabad: the excessive dependence of Christians upon mission employment, and the other difficulties of a rootless community. The Ohio Quakers, however, were not affected by the divergencies of outlook which appeared among Hoshangabad Friends; they concentrated on preaching the Gospel and seeking converts, and sometimes provoked active opposition. On one occasion hostile villagers had gathered to attack a preaching team while its members were meeting for prayer. A brave and gentle Muslim intervened and saved them, rebuking the villagers and reminding them of the Islamic teaching that those who disturbed men at their prayers incurred the displeasure of God. 'This was a common superstition,' wrote the missionaries in their report; they said nothing of the courage and good will that had been shown.

The difference in aims and outlook between the Ohio Friends and the British Quakers of the younger generation meant that there was little contact between the two groups, although some of the older British missionaries kept in touch and the much-loved Mary Allen gave unpretentious service in both areas. The Bundelkhand Quakers found a closer spiritual fellowship with other evangelical groups; the British Quakers were increasingly drawn, from 1920 onwards, to seek out those who recognised what Poornachandra had called 'the universal spiritual religion of God on earth' under its many differing outward forms. Indian thinkers themselves were calling on Quakers to do some bridge-building: 'Christianity should be *lived*, and Hindu mysticism made more practical. *Why don't the Quakers do it?*'[20]

XI

'Quaker Embassies'

To hold together faith and works, the sense of adora-
tion and the obligation of service, is an essential and
practicable task.

C. E. Raven,
The Theological Basis of Christian Pacifism

The spiritual upheaval of the First World War was all the more
devastating because so many had assumed, during the years which
had preceded it, that war was a thing of the past. The Society of
Friends stood firm in its peace testimony, though some of its peace
meetings in England were broken up by mob violence, and a
number of its young men were imprisoned for refusing to fight.
Many Quakers, both men and women, devoted themselves to the
relief of suffering on both sides of the conflict.

The experience compelled a radical rethinking of the principles
upon which human society should be based, for Quakers were
convinced that there could be no lasting peace without justice and
right relationships, between man and man and between nation and
nation. In 1920 the British and American Friends who had worked
together for the victims of war were instrumental in holding a world
conference in London to consider how Friends could act for peace
in the face of the world's need. The conference declared that 'peace
is not a policy, it is a conviction of the soul', and that to live out that
conviction, faithfully and fearlessly, would mean working for
fundamental and revolutionary social change.

One of the pioneers of the new thinking was Carl Heath, who was
to be a key figure in Quaker relations with India during the next
twenty-five years. He was born in 1869 and so was an exact contemporary of Mahatma Gandhi. He spent much of his boyhood among
radical thinkers in Paris; later, working as a teacher in London, he

became deeply concerned about the desperate poverty round about him. He was not then a Quaker, but like many of the young Quakers his contemporaries (and like Gandhi) he read Ruskin and Tolstoy and pondered their ideas. Like Martin Wood, he was involved in the European Peace Congresses held at the turn of the century, and after the Congress of 1908 he became Joint Secretary, along with Joseph Gundry Alexander, of the National Peace Council in Britain. In 1914 the Peace Council, whose appeal was to reason and common sense, was shattered by the emotions of war; only those stood firm for whom peace was 'a conviction of the soul'. Among them were the Quakers, and Carl Heath. He threw himself into Quaker work for war victims, joined the Society in 1916, and quickly became a leader.

Carl Heath at once began to urge that Quaker service for peace must deal with 'the whole range of international and social life' in a way which appealed not to expediency but to the power of the spirit of Christ. It must testify to 'a living reality which breaks down the barriers of race, nation and religion and binds men together in one divine life'. He envisaged this service as being focused in 'embassies of the City of God to every great city of man'. These Quaker embassies, settlements or outposts (as he variously called them) would present the Quaker message, religious and humanitarian, as one indivisible whole. 'Our settlements must stand first for the reality and universality of the divine indwelling, secondly for study and thirdly for service'; they must aim at 'the liberation of the Light in all'. He believed that such embassies were needed not only in the war-torn 'cities of man' in Europe but also in the divided, restless 'cities of man' in Asia.

Heath's thinking, with its emphasis on Life, was in line with the convictions which led British Quakers in 1921 to replace their old book, *Christian Doctrine*, by a book of Quaker religious experience named *Christian Life, Faith and Thought*. 'Life itself', stated the preface to the new book, 'is the way by which God has spoken and is still speaking.' Parallel developments were taking place in America, where in a number of yearly meetings the former emphasis on individual 'salvation' was being replaced by a sense of 'spiritual mission and social concern'.[1] The idea of 'Quaker embassies' met with an enthusiastic response; in the first years after the war Quakers, like many others, felt the urge to 'a new missionary movement' to proclaim afresh the message of 'peace on earth, good will among men'. The new missionary ideal, however, was far removed from the old, as Heath's words showed: 'Asians, from within their own indigenous pattern of thought and feeling, and in their own responsible communal framework, might learn at their own speed from Christian faith and insights, practical as well as mystical, as part of man's common religious heritage.' Heath was saying what the Calcutta Quakers had said thirty years before, that the task was to deepen the common awareness of what Tukaram had called 'God within humanity' and Poornachandra had thought of as 'the Gospel church of the Substance'. There should be no 'opting out' of the responsible framework of one's cultural environment.

Heath presented his plea for Quaker embassies to the London Yearly Meeting of 1917, with the support of Henry T. Hodgkin, the secretary of the FFMA. By a timely coincidence Joseph and Katherine Taylor, who had recently retired from their long service with the FFMA in Hoshangabad, laid before the same Yearly Meeting their long-standing concern to go to Calcutta, in response to that invitation which had first reached London in 1861. Both Heath and Hodgkin gave them warm support, and early in 1919, as soon as hostilities ceased and travel became possible, the Calcutta 'settlement' was begun.

In one sense, it was 'too late'. Poornachandra was dead, and the younger men and women whom he had attracted had been unable to maintain the Meeting for Worship without him. They welcomed the Taylors with friendliness and handed over the Quaker records and library books, but they did not join the new group – possibly its habitual use of English instead of their native Bengali created a barrier, especially for the women. The Taylors got in touch with other isolated Quakers in the city: Frederic Gravely of the Indian Museum; Nalin Ganguly, Brahmin scholar and 'gentle discerning spirit', who had become a Friend while headmaster of the Hoshangabad High School under Jack Hoyland, and had later joined the staff of the YMCA in his native Bengal;[2] Frank Squire, an Irish Friend in his early forties who had left his family business to help the depleted staff of the Calcutta YMCA during the difficult war years. These three introduced Indian friends, one of whom, N. J. Bose,[3] helped the Taylors to find a house in Beadon Street near the university. Frank Squire came to live with them, and devoted all his leisure hours to the work of the Centre.

Beadon Street was a decent unpretentious Bengali neighbourhood, well away from the wealthy 'British' residential area in south

Calcutta. The house itself, however, had formerly been the 'Beadon Bar Hotel', and had had a rather shady reputation. 'You have turned hell into heaven,' smiled a Bengali neighbour who called on the Taylors soon after they had settled in. The change was more than physical. 96 Beadon Street quickly became known: the door was open to all, and ordinary Indian people felt at home there, as they had done in the Quaker home at Prahlad Ghat fifty years before. Like the Beards, the Taylors cared about students, about the position of women, about public affairs in India and the world, about 'the Quaker interpretation of Christ's teaching'. Their morning silent worship was often joined by students and others; their Sunday evening lecture-forums might sometimes be 'swamped' by listeners; little groups met to study the Gospels. 'We all feel we are in the place of our Heavenly Father's appointing,' wrote Joseph happily.

As time went on other Friends and near-Friends found the Centre. Jack Clarke, who had served in the Friends Ambulance Unit during the war, arrived with his young wife to work for the YMCA, and another former FAU man, S. J. E. Virgo, joined the staff of one of the banks. An American Quaker family, William and Hazel Elliott and their children, were in the city, and a young Baptist missionary, Horace Collins, who had been a student at Woodbrooke. Collins's 'conviction of the soul' about the Christian way of peace was to make him a tower of strength to lonely pacifists in Calcutta during another world war twenty years later.

As in Benares, there was some initial Christian hostility, but 1920 was not 1870 and things soon changed. 'When you first came you were not wanted,' said a senior Indian Christian to Joseph Taylor. 'But I tell you frankly you have been a blessing; this house is the centre of unity and fellowship for us all.' Many Christians, both Indian and foreign, were impatient of sectarian divisions and shared the Quaker concern for peace. They found the Quaker home 'an oasis', and dreamed of a future Indian church where 'all the better things of Quakerism' should have a place. The Taylors sometimes pointed out the contrast between the generous respect shown them by the Oxford Mission (which put a high value on ritual and sacrament) and the unfriendly suspicion with which some Quakers in Britain regarded 'ritualists'. 'We have very good relations with *our friend the enemy*,' Joseph Taylor once wrote to London, 'but better not say so in a report!'* (See footnote page 120.)

The home in Beadon Street was valued at least as much by

spiritual seekers outside the churches. Nalin Ganguly was thinking chiefly of them when he wrote of the work of the settlement as 'a leavening process . . . a pioneer experiment in living permeation as distinct from mechanical organisation'.[4] He might have added that many such seekers, inspired by the poet-prophet Rabindranath Tagore, were being led into paths very close to the Quaker. 'I must know [God] by my own efforts' (i.e. not by second-hand report), wrote a young teacher at Santiniketan. 'He is . . . not to be reached except through the affections of men. We come into the world to create ourselves and we can do it only through love.' Another, who had met Jane Addams in the USA, wrote of 'the joy of finding the spirit of God, which is within each one but which can be unfolded only in fellowship'. He did not know her creed, he said; 'she belongs to the consecrated church of human brotherhood'.[5] There were sensitive spirits like these among the young people who came to the settlement. Frank Squire asked one of them why he did not declare himself a Christian. His reply was illuminating: 'Everyone knows that I love Christ and try to live like Jesus. But I must remain a true Hindu. I do not wish to have hatred in my heart as the English do against the Germans.'

Quakers could not live in the middle of Calcutta from 1919 to 1923 without experiencing the storms of political emotion and prejudice which marked those years. In 1919 Indian hopes of political advance had been bitterly disappointed; the Rowlatt Acts and the shooting at Amritsar were followed in 1920–1 by Gandhi's first non-cooperation movement and the Khilafat agitation, and then in 1922 by Gandhi's arrest and by the Moplah rebellion and its aftermath. Calcutta was in a state of almost continuous excitement and turmoil. In spite of Gandhi's condemnation of terrorism, hooligan elements were incited to indiscriminate violence against individual English people,[6] and police reprisals were sometimes equally indiscriminate. Beadon Square was a sort of local Hyde Park Corner where every Sunday evening demagogues stirred up racial hatred, while a few yards away the 'small peace garrison' of Quakers was trying to promote understanding and good will. When

---

* Forty years later a Quaker teacher from London, Fred Pinn, spent five years with the Oxford Mission building up a school where boys from the poorest homes learned 'to handle tools with skill, tackle jobs with confidence, and use their brains on their *real* problems'. It was education in the spirit of Penn and of Gandhi, but it was done in complete isolation from other Quakers in India.

passion was at its highest, Bengali neighbours invited the Quakers to take refuge in their homes if need should arise. Fortunately it never did.

It is not surprising that Joseph Taylor should have wished to revive the former Bombay *Guardian* as a vehicle of Quaker concern for public affairs. He had been interested from the outset in its potential as a 'metropolitan outlet' by which Quaker ideas might 'influence a continent'. In 1898 when the Dyers left the paper was in financial difficulty, but Taylor protested strongly against the decision to close it down, and his protest, backed by Pandita Ramabai, was heeded. Under the editorship of a young Quaker couple, Percy and Alice Horne, and their helper and successor Arthur J. Sharpe, the *Guardian* recovered its original breadth of outlook. It aimed 'to deal with all current topics from the standpoint of spiritual [Quaker] views of Christian truth and its testimony for peace and national righteousness', and did this in a way that was much appreciated.[7] After they left, however, it fell into the hands of some narrowly sectarian Bombay Protestants, who regarded questions of 'national righteousness' as 'quite different from the Gospel' and therefore outside their range of interest. It lost many readers, and in 1918 was obliged to close. The way was open for a new start, especially as the old organ of Christian opinion in Calcutta, *The Friend of India*, had also come to an end.

Joseph Taylor hoped at first to make the *Guardian* a definitely Quaker paper, 'a link in the chain of Quaker periodicals'. The *Guardian* trustees, however, had before them an alternative proposal that 'a wider basis' might be ensured by a merger with one or two other papers, such as the organ of the YMCA. Taylor hesitated to push his own plan because 'Quakers are so weak in securing continuity', but there were many frustrating delays, partly because the YMCA was troubled by political disagreements. In the end there was no merger, but it was not until January 1923 that the *Guardian*, directed by an independent Indian committee, could begin its new life. Taylor's first editorial was its manifesto: it would aim to interpret public affairs in the light of the teaching of Jesus, to champion the poor and oppressed, to promote racial and communal harmony. 'This paper is national,' wrote Taylor. 'It holds that the control of the administration of India should be placed in the hands of the people of India. . . . It stands for freedom – national, international, religious, social – which it believes to be a profoundly Christian thing.'

Joseph Taylor's associate editor, A. N. Sudarisanam, was a man of rare quality. As K. T. Paul's personal secretary, he had already gained much insight into conditions in many parts of India. At the time of the Moplah outbreak he had gone to Malabar, 'exercising a practical ministry of reconciliation in his quiet, firm but cheerful way'. The paper attracted some able contributors, and maintained a high standard of journalistic integrity and independence; it would never yield to party pressures or 'go off the gold standard' (as one of its friends expressed it). The editorial partnership lasted little more than a year, for in 1924 Joseph Taylor felt that the time had come to retire. Sudarisanam carried on in Calcutta for several years, with great courage and determination, and then in 1932 moved the paper to Madras. He remained editor for the next twenty years, until his comparatively early death in 1952. He had steady Quaker support, financial and personal, both in India and in Britain, and in his hands the *Guardian* won great respect as a vehicle of independent and radical Christian thought.[8]

We may share Joseph Taylor's regret that this enterprise could not have begun in 1920, for in those stormy years there would certainly have been a place for a mouthpiece of genuinely non-partisan opinion, not afraid 'to speak truth to power' on either side. Taylor's reports to London show that he was scrupulously fair, and thorough in his scrutiny of evidence. Much of what he says about the events of the time confirms the judgement of C. F. Andrews, for whose concern with the human face of politics he had a warm admiration. He saw the deeper significance of Gandhi as one who stood for 'the ancient ideal of the spiritual civilisation of India'; he watched with affectionate sympathy the student enthusiasts for whom Gandhi embodied 'the way of love taught by Jesus which is the way to freedom'.

During the same years another closely knit group of Friends had grown up in Madras. At the beginning of 1920 Frederic Gravely was appointed Superintendent of the Madras Government Museum, and found that Edward Barnes, a fellow scientist and near-Quaker, was already teaching in the Madras Christian College. The following year they were joined by two Quaker couples, Reginald and Freda Dann and Guy and Emily Jackson, and by William Hindle, another YMCA worker. This made it possible to have a regular Meeting for Worship, in which a number of 'friends of Friends', both Indian and Western, found a spiritual home; some of them joined the Society, while during the years that followed a number of other Quakers lived in the city for shorter or longer periods and added their strength to the group.

Madras, like Calcutta, felt the political stress of the times. The Quakers gave strong support to an Indian initiative in reconciliation, the Madras International Fellowship. This was founded in 1922 and was open to men and women of any race, creed or political colouring on a basis of 'faith in God and the practice of silence'. It brought together 'non-cooperators' and government servants, Indians and Englishmen (and many other nations), Hindus, Muslims, Parsees, Christians, to enjoy 'multilingual volley-ball, intercommunal tennis, cosmopolitan tea-parties, and discussion'. 'Some say it is unnecessary, others that it is impossible,' reported its devoted and energetic founder-secretary, A. A. Paul.[9] In the eyes of many it was both necessary and possible. Guy Jackson, as a civil engineer in Madras government service, was periodically transferred from one town to another; wherever they lived he and Emily helped to found new fellowships. Others were started in other parts of India, and by 1927 groups as distant from one another as Lahore in the north and Trivandrum in the far south had been linked with a score of others in a federation; the Council of the Federation met in Gandhi's ashram at Sabarmati with his blessing and guidance.

Friends in India gained much from their work with the Fellowship. Among those who met Quakers through these interests were Alice (Varley) Barnes and Doris (Hitchcock) Chetsingh, both of whom were to do much for Quakers in India in later years. Professor P. A. Wadia of Bombay, the Chairman of the Council of the Federation, also became a close 'friend of Friends'. Although he never formally joined the Society, his home in central Bombay was for years the venue of a Quaker meeting for worship of which he himself was a faithful member, and whose quiet power is still gratefully remembered.[10] Bombay Friends like Kathleen Whitby and Agnes Maclean gave much valued service both in the city and elsewhere.

The Quaker settlement in Calcutta undertook as part of its service the maintaining of friendly contacts between the scattered Quakers who were in India for business or professional work. Quite a number of such Friends had lived in India in earlier periods, but as we have seen they had almost always been isolated from one another and from such organised Quaker groups as existed. The

Taylors did a lot to bring this isolation to an end, and from 1920
onwards the value of some form of Indian Quaker fellowship was
recognised. Jack Clarke and Stanley Virgo were not the only
ex-FAU men to find their way to India. Another, George McCabe,
was working on a co-operative farm in rural Bengal, and two more,
Hugh Maclean and William Pitt, were in Dehra Dun. Jack Hoyland
returned to India towards the end of 1919 to join the staff of the
Hislop College, Nagpur, where he worked for the next eight years.
In Nagpur also were Robert and Margaret Pearl (on a research
assignment), an American Friend, H. H. Peterson, and Shiv Ram, a
Gurkha convert who after a period at Kingsmead had returned to
India eager to help Indian Christians to achieve self-reliance
through co-operative enterprise, and had worked with Jack at
Hoshangabad. Both these men, like so many other Quakers at the
time, were working for the YMCA.[11] Another of Jack Hoyland's
near-contemporaries, Percy Oddie Whitlock, had joined the Indian
Educational Service in 1914 and was teaching in Cuttack, while his
brother-in-law, Henry King, was a member of a firm of architects in
Bombay. Theodore Burtt, who had made friends with Nalin Ganguly when they were both students in Birmingham, had become an
irrigation engineer in the Punjab; Charles Terrell's son was a doctor
in Assam, Hubert Walker a tea-planter in the same area. All these,
along with the Madras Friends and a good many of those in the
Hoshangabad area, were part of an incipient Quaker fellowship
which also included the men and women of various religious backgrounds who associated with them in the major towns.

But when the time came for Joseph and Katherine Taylor to leave
Calcutta there was, as Joseph had feared, no one to ensure the
continuation of the work they had begun. In March 1924 the house
in Beadon Street was given up, and the Quaker fellowship in Calcutta withered away. For all the breadth and promise of its outreach
the settlement had had no local roots. Nalin Ganguly, rooted as he
was in Bengali Hindu culture, might have been able to build on the
preceding indigenous Quaker movement, but he was absent in
England during the critical years 1919–21, and when he returned to
his work in the YMCA he had little spare time. By the end of 1922
nearly all the foreign Quakers had left Calcutta for various reasons.
Frank Squire and his wife remained for some years, but like Nalin
he had commitments which left him no time to act as a focus for
Quaker interests in India as the Taylors had begun to do.[12]

At this juncture Carl Heath approached the Madras Friends. Was there not, he asked, the potential for a Quaker Centre in Madras? They replied that reconciling service was needed there as everywhere, but that they could not do more than they were already doing without a full-time worker, who should be familiar with the local language and culture. That was what had been lacking in Calcutta. The Madras Quakers seem also to have felt the need, in the vacuum left by the Taylors' withdrawal, for a reconsideration of Quaker service in India as a whole. In 1925 they held a quiet consultation among themselves, at which the then President of the Servants of India Society, V. Srinivasa Sastri, was present, and proposed that there should be an all-India Quaker conference to consider what the right next step should be.

Among the workers in the Hoshangabad District there was also a sense of the need for a new start. It was not enough, said some of the younger missionaries, 'to drift along like a wreck of the pre-war mission'; they too wanted to think out their calling in India afresh. In the Mid-India Yearly Meeting, now beginning to assume responsibility for the direction of its own affairs, there were those who shared the longing for a renewal of spiritual vision and purpose. 'Our people know the Christ of the New Testament; what they need is the *living* Christ,' said one of them. When Hugh Maclean arrived in India in 1919 he found groups of young people from Itarsi and Khera meeting 'in fields and desert places' to seek together the guidance of the Spirit.[13] A conference such as Madras proposed might have enabled all these threads of Quaker concern to be brought together – not perhaps at once, for the differences of background, outlook and language were formidable, but by providing some framework within which understanding might have grown.

The conference, however, was never held. None of the Madras Friends was free to undertake the task of organising it, and Jack Hoyland, who also had the vision and the concern, was carrying a tremendous daily burden of teaching and administration. He was also writing prolifically – the *Prayers for use in an Indian College* will not soon be forgotten – and spending himself to the full in making friends with his passionately nationalist students and leading them in service to Gond villages stricken by cholera and famine. Francis Kilbey, whose reports on the non-cooperation movement in the Hoshangabad area in 1921–2 were as positive and fair-minded as

Joseph Taylor's,* had retired 'to make room for younger people'; his friend Geoffrey Maw, it would seem, did not feel called to initiate the kind of consultation which Madras proposed, although he did his best to maintain contact with Friends all over India in the way that Joseph Taylor had done.

In the absence of any lead such as a conference in India might have given, the Council for International Service began to promote visits to India by British 'Quaker ambassadors', not in order to staff a centre, but to express Quaker good will towards India and to give the Quaker message in the spirit of Carl Heath. A number of well-known British Quakers carried out lecture tours, meeting with intellectuals and students in many cities and speaking of Quaker religious principles, the testimony to peace and 'the politics of human brotherhood'. In 1926 the American Quaker Rufus M. Jones, on his way home to the United States from China, paid a similar visit to some of the university centres, including Nagpur, and urged that Carl Heath's vision of 'a chain of vital centres' should be made a reality. His visit stimulated Jack Hoyland and Harold Peterson to work out some specific proposals, one of which concerned the need for 'bridges of understanding' between India's divided religious communities. Some years earlier, with his own students in mind, Jack had prepared a booklet on *Gita, Gospel and Quran*,[14] and some of the finest of the Indian leaders agreed that 'there will never be real Hindu-Muslim unity till each tries to understand the other's religion and culture'.[15]

At this juncture Peterson, then working near Lahore, received a letter from the American Quaker Thomas Kelly, telling of his deep concern for 'a brotherhood relationship in the joint search for Truth' with 'people of *all* religions who lift up hands in prayer'. Hoyland at once proposed that Thomas Kelly should come to India and with Nalin Ganguly create a new centre. Kelly's conception of the Divine Incarnation as 'not an isolated fact occurring once [but] the fundamental basis of all human lives . . . a world process in which God eternally re-clothes himself in humanity' was surely one which would find a response in India. Part of the centre's work, Hoyland urged, ought to be the serious study of Hindu-Muslim relations; let this be led by an American rather than an Englishman – the latter would be suspect, he feared, in such a sensitive area.[16]

---

* Kilbey spoke warmly of the increased understanding of 'non-violence' among ordinary people. He also queried the haste with which some officials accused 'agitators' of deliberately starting forest fires, when 'every cooly in the forest service smokes'!

Although nothing came of this proposal, it is of great interest that just about this time a British Quaker, Ernest Ludlam, who was then teaching at Edinburgh University, was asked informally whether he could find a Quaker educationist who would be willing to serve in the Aligarh Muslim University.[17] It is possible that the request was an outcome of the lecture tour undertaken by John William Graham, who had been a fellow student at Cambridge of Theodore Beck and Philip Sturge, and had in consequence had a warm welcome both at Aligarh and at the Nizam's College, Hyderabad. Ernest Ludlam was unable to find a suitable recruit, and it is hard not to feel that an opportunity both for study and for reconciling service may have been missed. During the next fateful twenty years the Quakers chiefly active in Indian affairs seem to have taken less care than they might have done to 'keep their friendships in repair' among Indian Muslims, especially those whose political outlook differed from Gandhi's. Fellow Quakers who in the thirties criticised their 'one-sidedness' were not altogether wrong. American Friends sometimes made similar mistakes. A reading-list prepared by the AFSC for prospective workers in India in 1947 – the year when mounting political distrust culminated in the partition of the country amid appalling suffering for the innocent – did not contain a single book on a Muslim subject or by a Muslim author.

Jack Hoyland's second proposal was that the steps towards the integration of all Quaker witness and service in India which had been taken by the Quaker settlement in Calcutta should be followed up. The land at Rasulia had been lying unused since the Industrial Works had closed in 1918; could it not become 'an Indian Woodbrooke', he asked, a centre of study and religious fellowship, with very simple accommodation such as was being provided by the various Gandhian and Christian ashrams in India? By offering a library and book centre, and a varied programme of summer schools, youth camps, retreats and study courses, it might interpret both the religious dimension and the social concern of Quakerism, as indivisible aspects of the one 'divine Life', in the way that Carl Heath envisaged. Perhaps the *Guardian* (then struggling for its life in Calcutta) might under the auspices of such a centre become a vehicle of *Quaker* commentary on public affairs as Joseph Taylor would have liked it to be.

Seen from a distance of fifty years that seems a timely proposal. An 'Indian Woodbrooke' led by someone like Jack Hoyland who knew both the Hoshangabad District and the larger aspects of

Indian society might have given the members of Mid-India Yearly
Meeting an opportunity to break out of their isolation and to study
the Quaker religious and humanitarian traditions side by side with
other inquirers and spiritual seekers of many kinds. It might have
offered rebels against social, economic and political injustice a
chance to learn of the dynamics of change, both in the Quaker past
and the Indian present. It might have helped scattered, isolated
Quakers all over the country to feel that their own concerns were
part of a larger enterprise. And external conditions were favourable; the railway connection through Nagpur to Madras was just
coming into operation, and Hoshangabad was more accessible than
ever from all sides; in London the Friends Service Council had just
taken over the responsibilities both of the Council for International
Service and the FFMA, and was therefore in a position to look at
Quaker relationships with India as one whole.

More important than such externals, however, was the India-
wide challenge to all that the 'Quaker embassies' stood for. They
were founded on a 'conviction of the soul' that, as the first Quakers
had declared, the spirit of Christ would never sanction the use of
outward weapons in any cause, however righteous, and that the
social and international justice which they knew to be essential to
peace must be fought for with 'the sword of the spirit' alone. It was
this conviction that had made Quakers respond so warmly to the
open truthfulness and non-violence of Gandhi's principles of action.
But in 1927–8 the youth of India no longer followed Gandhi as they
had done a few years earlier. They were angry and humiliated.
'India has been told', wrote Fred Gravely, 'that because she cannot
defend herself she has no right to independence.' The result was a
loud demand by students for compulsory military training in the
universities. Therefore, continued Gravely, while the Quaker peace
witness was as relevant as ever, 'it would need to be on quite
different lines from that in the West'.[18] Could an 'Indian Woodbrooke' have inspired study and action to meet that need?[19] Such
questions remained unanswered. Jack Hoyland himself was unable
for health reasons to remain in India, and no other Quaker felt that
quickening of personal concern which had taken the Taylors to
Calcutta. Nevertheless, if the vision of an 'Indian Woodbrooke'
could have been presented not as the dream of one man, however
knowledgeable and concerned, but as the considered proposal of an
all-India Quaker conference (as it well might have been) it might
have had more serious attention.

Meanwhile, however, events in the political field were moving British Quakers to establish somewhat different priorities. The Government of India Act of 1919 contained a provision that the working of the constitution should be reviewed after ten years, and in this connection a Parliamentary Commission headed by Sir John Simon was appointed to visit India. None of its members was Indian, none had Indian experience, and the purpose of the visit was not made clear to the Indian public. It seemed to politically conscious Indians that the British Government was still clinging to its old attitude, 'We know best what is good for you', and they were naturally irritated and resentful.[20] All the major political groups in India, including the 'moderates', were united in refusing their co-operation to the Commission. There were renewed efforts to reach agreement among themselves with regard to the issues which divided them.

It was at this time, in 1927–8, that Horace G. Alexander paid his first visit to India. He was nearing his fortieth year, and was lecturing in international affairs at Woodbrooke; for some years he had worked with C. F. Andrews over the opium traffic, whose abuses his father, J. G. Alexander, had investigated more than thirty years before. In India he met with Andrews's closest friends, Tagore and Gandhi, with whom he laid the foundations of a lasting friendship; with Fred Gravely he attended the meetings of the Indian National Congress in Madras. His experiences during this whole tour convinced him of the urgency of persuading the British Government and people to take a new attitude towards India, an attitude of genuine respect and trust which would enable Indians speedily to assume real responsibility for their own affairs. Carl Heath and many others shared his concern, and the Friends Service Council resolved that Quakers ought as a body to 'face political issues', and to seek to promote mutual respect and conciliation between the rival interests, and particularly between India and Britain.

During the next few years came the Round Table Conferences in London on the future government of India, and the personal contacts with Tagore and Gandhi which many Quakers enjoyed during the visits of the Indian leaders to Britain in 1930 and 1931. In 1929 Horace Alexander had encouraged a younger Friend, Reginald Reynolds, to visit India, and on his return Reynolds made many young Quakers vividly aware of the moral dimensions of India's struggle for freedom; Friends as a whole followed the events in India after Gandhi's arrest early in 1932 with increasing anxiety.

Carl Heath became chairman of an India Conciliation Group which involved a number of Friends in the political issues along with other concerned Englishmen such as C. F. Andrews and Henry Polak, Gandhi's old friend from South Africa. Quaker visitors to India in the thirties, unlike those of the twenties, concentrated less on universities and intellectuals than on the centres of political power. It would be hard to speak too highly of the untiring devotion of Horace Alexander, Carl Heath and other Quaker leaders.[21] In spite of the comparative failure, as suggested earlier, to win the full confidence of some powerful political figures (Hindu as well as Muslim), they caught the imagination of the Indian people and laid the foundation of a good will towards Quakers which has constantly been renewed.

The Quaker openness during this period to Indian initiatives, and the close collaboration with C. F. Andrews, led to a new development. Instead of working only in Quaker-planned institutions or schemes, Quakers were 'seconded' and sometimes supported for service under Indian leadership in Indian organisations. One result of Horace Alexander's visit to Tagore at his educational centre at Santiniketan was the appointment of Nalin Ganguly to take charge of the developing college department there. In harmony with the Quaker testimony to sexual equality, he established a wholesome and successful pattern of coeducation. A year or two later, through the attraction of Tagore's ideas and the friendship of C. F. Andrews, a young American Quaker couple, Dr Harry Timbres and his wife Rebecca, joined the medical staff of Tagore's Rural Service Department, where in a few years Harry made a valuable contribution to the understanding (and therefore the control) of the incidence of malaria in West Bengal. This pattern of Quaker service has continued ever since, while the Quaker-planned institutions themselves have become more and more closely linked, through cooperation in common tasks and through exchange of workers, with Indian initiatives for national service.[22]

Much significant work in this field has been done by Rasulia, which was reopened in the mid-thirties not as an 'Indian Wood-brooke' but as a Friends rural settlement. The pioneer was Hilda Cashmore, who was one of a Quaker team which visited India amid the bitter political resentments of 1932. She had already given distinguished service both in Quaker relief work during the war and in urban 'settlements' involved in social tensions in England. The Rasulia Rural Settlement, in her view, might offer Indian and

English workers a chance to work together on a basis of equality, both in study and in practical service. A meeting for worship, a library, and an outpost for service in the needy forest hamlet of Jamai reflected Carl Heath's threefold ideal. The settlement attracted the leaders of the town and captured the imagination of students; Banwarilal Chaudhuri, the son of a local farmer, attended one of Hilda Cashmore's student camps, at which C. F. Andrews was also present, and has devoted himself ever since to the welfare of Indian villages under the double inspiration of Gandhi and the Quakers, and in continuous friendly co-operation with the Rasulia Settlement.

Hilda Cashmore felt strongly that the settlement should demonstrate Quaker faith in Indian leadership, and she succeeded in getting Ranjit Chetsingh to take her place. Ranjit and his English wife Doris had joined the Friends a few years before;[23] his special interest was in education at all levels, and during his years at Rasulia he introduced Gandhi's ideas of basic education into village schools and helped to pioneer adult education on an all-India scale. He also, like Joseph Taylor and Geoffrey Maw, realised the value of an all-India Quaker fellowship, and in December 1939, under the shadow of the Second World War, the first conference of 'scattered Friends' from various parts of the country met at Rasulia. Other gatherings followed, in which Quakers shared with equally concerned followers of Gandhi in a common search for right ways of practising love and non-violence in a time of war. The meetings were held in a spirit which made possible great depth and openness, recognising the areas both of unity and of difference.

As the political situation grew more tense with the 'Quit India' movement of 1942 and the simultaneous military threat from Japan, Ranjit felt led to undertake a new task: the establishment of what Joseph Taylor would have called a 'peace garrison', among the stresses of Delhi. The Delhi Quaker Centre came into being in 1943, to provide a meeting-place, 'permeated by Christian values and the Quaker spirit', to which all open-minded people of good will might come, and find understanding and co-operation in overcoming the hatreds and evil passions of the time. Another Quaker enterprise had already begun in Calcutta, where in 1942, in view of the war situation, the Friends Ambulance Unit established a small but experienced team. Horace Alexander's leadership made it possible for the team to work with government officials and at the same time with the blessing of Gandhi and the co-operation of Indians of

every political colouring. This widespread trust and good will was
the basis of effective service in the disasters which were to follow –
the destructive cyclone of October 1942, the famine of 1943, and
the outbursts of partisan fury which preceded and followed the
partition of the country in 1947, and which overwhelmed both
Calcutta and Delhi.

It did not prove possible to find another Indian leader to follow
the Chetsinghs at Rasulia; their place was taken by Donald and
Erica Groom, who had already been in Hoshangabad for three
years as workers for the Friends Service Council. Donald and Erica
were among the many young Quakers whose interest in India had
been awakened by Gandhi and all that he stood for. During those
years Mary Barr, a former missionary in Hyderabad State, who had
found that Gandhi 'interpreted Christ to her in a new way', was
living in a village not far away and working out Gandhian
programmes. She herself joined Friends, and a succession of young
people, Quakers and others, worked in the village with her. Many of
those whom the Friends Service Council sent to the Hoshangabad
District as teachers, doctors or nurses also believed that they should
work for the benefit of the whole local community, not specially for
Christians. They did not want to make the Mid-India Yearly Meeting the centre of their interest, still less did they want to
'proselytise'. They were suspicious of 'missions' and were attracted
by Gandhi's saying that the fragrance of a truly religious life, like the
fragrance of a rose, needs no preaching to commend it. They made
friends less easily among the local Mid-India Friends than among
the Congressmen and others who shared their outlook on public
affairs.

Donald Groom tried to do with local Friends what Jack Hoyland
had done on a smaller scale with his students – get them to participate along with others in projects of community service. 'Instead of
concentrating on serving the small group of Friends,' he wrote, 'I
sought to associate them with people of different religions or none
in . . . a spiritual fellowship of service to the whole rural community.
This was the path to the strengthening of faith and a challenge to its
reality.'[24] True, but the 'free and fearless education' which might
have enabled the mid-India Quakers to respond to the challenge
had so far been lacking. Perhaps the want might have been supplied
if Quakers had given priority to establishing an Indian Quaker
ashram of the kind Jack Hoyland had envisaged, which might have
offered opportunities of meaningful, disciplined and consecrated

study, religious and secular, unhampered by the limitations of the ordinary schools.

But, as things were, the Mid-India Yearly Meeting was not yet ready to enter into these wider concerns. The Grooms at Rasulia developed comprehensive and imaginative projects of community service, and became more and more closely involved, with other ex-patriate Quakers, in Gandhian programmes of various kinds. The local Indian Quakers unfortunately remained somewhat isolated from the concern for national welfare which found expression in the activities of the new Quaker centres in Delhi, Calcutta and Rasulia itself, although there were always some who tried to bridge the gap. The difficulties were not superficial. The mid-India Quakers, through no fault of their own, had little understanding either of the Indian cultural heritage or of the Quaker experience of a saving Light 'shining through all'; they thought of the Light of the Spirit as known only to Christians. A spiritual fellowship with people of other religions was for them a strange idea; but their fears and hesitations might gradually have been overcome if the British Quakers, instead of criticising their 'narrowness', had talked over the differences of outlook in the relaxed atmosphere of leisured personal friendship. Did some of those who busied themselves so strenuously with 'service' programmes need to take to heart the element of truth in the comment made in another context to ex-patriate Quakers in Delhi in 1949: 'Why do all you Englishmen wear yourselves out trying to reform us? Put first things first; sit down and make friends, like the Chetsinghs'?

There was one kind of service in which all were united: the response to the needs of the sick. A concern for public health in some form or other has been a feature of both the Quaker missions, and of nearly all the projects with which Friends have been concerned in independent India. The Friends Hospital in Itarsi, which had been working faithfully for over twenty years, was reorganised and expanded in the years following 1936 by an able and enthusiastic couple, William and Molly Tandy, and Barbara Hartland's coming made possible the training of nurses there. They and their successors, British and Indian, provided useful and sometimes outstanding service. After India became independent other Christian bodies in the area, and also the State Government, were associated in the management of the hospital, which now serves Itarsi as a government institution.

The Bundelkhand Quakers had been equally sensitive to medical needs. Esther Baird was a nurse, and after a few years a woman doctor had joined her in Nowgong; the Maharajah of Alipur gave them land for a dispensary, and other local rulers helped in various ways. The Maharajah of Chhatarpur, educated as a boy by Theodore Beck's friend Theodore Morison, understood the value of a hospital. In 1921 he asked Esther if the mission could provide one, and gave a generous grant of land for the purpose. Esther did not find it easy to raise the money; she commented wryly that many Ohio Friends would rather build churches than hospitals! It was nearly ten years before the hospital could be opened, but it soon earned and maintained a fine reputation, and its staff have also given valuable help to a Christian hospital in Nepal. It continues to work under Christian management and is a member of the Emmanuel Hospital Association of evangelical Christian hospitals.

In spite of Carl Heath's insistence that the religious and the humanitarian witness of Quakerism is one indivisible whole, Friends in India do tend to think of 'mission' and 'service' as separate categories of activity. The Bundelkhand Quakers, who joined in the emergency relief work during the Bihar drought of 1964, wrote in their report: 'We do undertake projects of social service, and we want to learn how to do it better in the name and spirit of Jesus Christ. . . . We are also [committed] to preach and teach the Gospel of Jesus Christ, to the end that people may be born anew into the Kingdom of God.' Let us set side by side with that statement Carl Heath's declaration that Quakers are called 'to share both the interior experience and the prophetic passion for social justice', for both the parallels and the differences between the two are relevant for Quakers and India today.

The humanitarian service *is* religious, 'prophetic', a witness to 'the spirit of Christ'; because it is that, it is part of the 'indivisible whole'. But for Carl Heath and for many of the Quakers whose service in India has been described it includes much more than first aid to the victims of disaster or injustice. It is a passion for righteousness in the very structures of society, and therefore it means wrestling with problems more difficult than first aid, in situations where conflicting interests each hold to some *partial* truth, precious but incomplete. For that reason *study*, the costly effort to grasp the *full* reality of a situation, is an essential element in effective response. Of Carl Heath's threefold programme for Quaker 'embassies' – witness, study, service – it is study that has most often been inadequate.

What of the Quaker witness to the 'interior experience'? Is it a one-way traffic of 'preaching and teaching', or a two-way traffic of 'sharing'? Quakers in India have differed on this point, and still do. They do not seem to differ about the essential nature of the inward experience itself; it is one of being 'born anew', or (in Horace Alexander's words) being 'turned from darkness to light, from fear to faith, from self to service'. Is not that the experience of *all* living religion? The lives which have known it carry the fragrance of which Gandhi spoke, and their outward religious labels are irrelevant. The beloved Eric Robertson of Rasulia, one of those who most successfully bridged the gap of communication between the centre and its Indian Quaker neighbours, had come to that new birth (as he delighted to witness) through the Gospel of Jesus Christ. But it was he who commented that the imagery of being 'born anew' is most meaningful when one remains *within* the organic human community of one's physical birth. That is exactly what Poornachandra had said more than fifty years before; Indian Quakers, and Indian friends of Quakers, have made the same point, in various ways, in each generation. The Kingdom of the new birth, the Kingdom of God, transcends our human boundary lines.

XII

Points of View

In the Spirit in whose living white radiance
    are blended all the colours of the world,
Who is the beginning and the end,
Who unites all humanity in goodwill and purified desire,
    May we be brought together and made one.

    Vedic chant, as quoted by Harry Timbres from Santiniketan, 1931

Just as the experience of the First World War had called out fresh thinking in Britain and America about the Quaker peace witness, so the experiences of 1942–7 called out similar thinking among those in India. The Quaker conference in 1920 had met in London and had been overwhelmingly 'white' in racial composition; the World Peace Meeting of 1949 was initiated by Quakers from India in consultation with Gandhi and some of his close associates. It met at Tagore's Santiniketan and then at Gandhi's Sevagram; it was far from exclusively Quaker, and Asia and Africa, and above all India, were as strongly represented as the West. In 1920 Quakers had glimpsed the truth that 'fundamental social changes' were a condition of lasting peace. By 1949 they had learned much from India of the *kind* of changes needed. Geoffrey Carnall described the vision in the Indian Quaker news-sheet *The Friendly Way*, in language whose rhythmic movement shows how deeply it had stirred him:

The hope of a new kind of social order,
undominated and undominating,
respectful in its treatment of man and beast
and in its use of the gifts of the earth,
is still not beyond the power of India to show
to an unbalanced and war-stricken world.

Quakers had also become aware that this hope had to be embodied not only in international political programmes but also in a *personal* witness, such as Gandhi had made by the way he lived, to the values of a peaceful society. 'There is no way to peace, peace *is* the way,' they said.

'Ideas have legs', they cross the frontiers of space and time, and it is not often possible to date their first appearance or trace the course of their development. There are three such ideas relevant to India's struggle for an 'undominating' social order, one or other of which have influenced much of the Quaker interchange with India during this century. The first is that each family should have an independent honest means of livelihood; the second that the conditions of life should make for optimum health; the third that in every human community there should be provision for the nourishment of the mind and the spirit.

'We need to remember', wrote Robin Hodgkin in 1976, 'the Franciscan and Gandhian notion that work with your hands, which is honest, has a profound meaning-generating power.' He was speaking of ways in which Quaker International Conferences in India might reach a deeper level of encounter than the intellectual. It has been largely forgotten that in 1919 two young Quakers, Hugh Maclean and William Pitt, came to India to give their Quaker witness through working with their hands, not just during a conference, but as a regular means of livelihood, as they would have done in England.

Hugh was a practical farmer, and William had worked under him in the agricultural section of the Friends Ambulance Unit. Their first idea was to earn their living by farming in the Dehra Dun area; but they could not get land at a fair price, and started a leather business in Dehra Dun instead. They rented an empty garage in the bazaar as a workshop and found workmen among the traditional shoemakers, Muslims and low-caste *mochis*. They quickly felt at home.

'We work alongside our men from 8.30 to 5,' wrote Hugh, 'sewing, cutting or making patterns, trying to live a Christian life at our daily work.' Their failure to get land, they decided, was a good thing. 'The leather business has taught us so much that we needed to learn, not only the skills of the trade. It has enabled us to look at things from an Indian point of view.' They learned an affectionate respect for their hard-working, teachable workmen, though some of them were 'notorious drunkards'. 'One thing has come home to me very forcibly,' Hugh continued, speaking of them. 'There are many who are "born of God" outside the Christian community.'

Dehra Dun was a considerable town, and the two young men made a good impression. The poorer 'Europeans' and pensioners appreciated their honest workmanship and moderate prices. Straight and open business practice had its own effect. 'Several shop-keepers have come after dark and told us that we have been a blessing to them. We do not know how.' Some of the Dehra Dun missionaries were critical of the meetings for worship which they held in their home, because they did not preach or press for an external 'conversion'. They had their answer: 'We believe that when the Lord said that the true believers would be his witnesses, he meant that their *lives* would speak.' All the same, like Rachel Metcalfe, they were ready to 'speak a word in season'. 'Although God does speak in the heart,' they reported, 'men like to hear a human voice, and they say, please come again.'

The little business paid its way, but it was too small to make the profit needed to pay for occasional visits to Britain. Yet they did not want to enlarge it, for then personal contacts would be lost and 'the spiritual drowned in the commercial'. By the end of 1920 the nationwide political unrest was also affecting personal relationships. Maclean and Pitt were in full sympathy with Indian aspirations, but the workshop was not as happy as it had been. It seemed that the time had come to move.

In the spring of 1921 Hugh explored the Kumaon hills, whose beauty reminded him happily of the Scotland of his boyhood. He found a community of skilled farmers, 'living entirely on the produce of their fields and orchards', who welcomed him and readily agreed to let him have land at a fair price. But just as the prospect seemed full of hope, he fell critically ill with typhoid fever. George McCabe, who had been one of his students in the FAU, came to help William through the crisis; Hugh's recovery was very slow, and he and William realised, sadly, that the plan for a Kumaon farm would have to be given up. For a time they worked on the staff of Dr Graham's Homes at Kalimpong in the eastern Himalayas; by 1924 they were back in England.

Such down-to-earth labour was not the only way in which expatriate Quakers have earned 'an honest livelihood' in India. There were others who 'spread the Truth in connection with their ordinary businesses'[1] and who found this most satisfying when the business itself was related to one or other of the three aspects of good community life which have been mentioned. Not every Quaker in India, of course, was a 'Quaker ambassador'; for a few, the pressure of 'the world's' standards proved too strong. But there were a number whose lives contributed to the Quaker–India dialogue in a way which is sometimes unrecorded in Quaker documents because it was not part of any 'official' corporate Quaker enterprise.

The first of these unofficial twentieth-century Quakers was Fred Gravely. His Quaker home and education had encouraged his strong bent towards natural history, but it was through his university connections, not through Friends, that the opening in the Indian Museum, Calcutta, was suggested to him in 1909. During his first years he carried out original biological research for his doctorate; apart from this satisfaction he was very happy in India, for he disregarded the conventional social hierarchies and made friends in all walks of Calcutta life. When war broke out in 1914 he found an avenue of pacifist service by taking charge of destitute boys of many races and religions in the home run by the 'Old Mission Church' in the city. In the time he could spare from his museum work he introduced them to the joys and skills of scouting; they gave him a lifelong interest in the needs of poor and despised groups, especially those of mixed or alien racial origin. But he knew nothing of Poornachandra and his Quaker group, and had no Quaker fellowship until Squire arrived in Calcutta in 1917 and they were both involved in the plans for the Quaker centre.

Before the centre had completed its first year, however, Gravely had left Calcutta. He was appointed Superintendent of the Government Museum in Madras; the scientific integrity and enthusiasm, and the concern for right human relationships, which pervaded his official work there for the next twenty-one years were an inseparable part of his Quaker witness. High scientific standards had been there before, but previous superintendents had tended to run the museum as a one-man show. It was Gravely who transformed its staff into a team who worked together for a common purpose: to advance knowledge of the natural and cultural environment of the people of South India and to enable the people themselves to understand, enjoy and respect the web of life and history around them. Gravely's own special contribution, apart from his unobtrusive leadership, was the enthusiasm with which he pioneered the hitherto neglected study of South-Indian temple architecture; his popular lectures on 'How to look at a temple' were much appreciated. His lasting visible memorial is the Archaeological Gallery where visitors have before them 'in a way that they can readily understand', the historical pageant of India's magnificent stone and bronze sculpture.

'We have tried to emulate Dr Gravely', wrote Professor T. N. Sadasivan, speaking for himself and a fellow scientist, 'in scientific ethics and in public relations. We know of no one we would rather resemble, as a man and as a scientist.' 'As a man' Gravely carried on in Madras the interests of his Calcutta days. For the first five years he was still a bachelor, and the quarters allocated to the Museum Superintendent 'were turned into a regular Scout Camp', where boys learned to waterproof their own groundsheets, or to cook a tasty meal out of doors in a maximum of one hour. The Scouts were not orphans, but Brahmin boys of good family, some of whom still remember those years of formative friendship.[2]

The story that Gravely once counted out the sticks in a box of matches in order to impress on his staff the need for scrupulous care in the use of resources derived from the taxes of the *poor*, would surely have appealed to Gandhi! For the poor and despised were never forgotten, and differences of race, creed or political outlook only made friendships, for Gravely, more interesting. In later years he was a regular visitor at the Madras Penitentiary, where he, government servant as he was, won the affectionate confidence of some of the government's political detainees, while he also gave all the spiritual strength of a lifetime of faithfulness to help prisoners under sentence of death. Gravely as a 'senior' Madras official disregarded the conventions as readily as he had done as a junior in Calcutta. In short, he did simply and directly what he thought right.

After Gravely married his Danish wife, Laura Balling, in 1925 their home became a focus of fellowship for the Madras Quakers whose work was described in the last chapter. From the very first, Gravely had found a kindred spirit in Edward Barnes, who was Professor of Chemistry in the Madras Christian College. 'Ted' Barnes combined a scrupulous intellectual honesty with a shy friendliness whose quality enriched both the Quaker Meeting for Worship and the International Fellowship. He was an enthusiastic amateur botanist, and he played a large part, along with the museum's botanical staff, in the preparation of a comprehensive and valuable survey of Madras flowering plants. After his marriage he and Alice Barnes became 'pioneer' settlers on the new site of the college in the scrub jungle outside the city. Ted's 'memorial' is in the hundreds of trees which shade the college roads, grown from seed-lings which he nursed and nurtured, planted and guarded until they could stand alone. Thanks to him too the patches of scrub which remained grew into tangles of fragrant wilderness, the mere thorns cut out, the things of beauty saved, by accurate knowledge and many hours of patient labour. Alice, who survived Ted by many years, gave much to Quakers in India through the warmth of her gift of friendship, and by her faithful editing, along with Mary Barr, of the Indian Quaker magazine *The Friendly Way*.[3]

Gravely and Barnes expressed their Quaker attitudes through work which nourished the mind and spirit, and helped to awaken respect for human achievement, for beauty and for truth. When Reginald Dann was appointed Director of Town Planning in Mad-ras in 1921 he added another dimension to these. He had great gifts, and from a worldly point of view he turned his back on a promising career when he left London for an Indian provincial city. From his own, Quaker, point of view there could be few more valuable contributions to the welfare of India than to help to plan homes adequate for family life in a city which made provision for the education, recreation and community interests of its citizens, and whose setting of natural beauty was preserved and cherished. There were, inevitably, many bureaucratic frustrations; Dann's dream of 'Madras Beautiful' was not realised, though some of his far-sighted plans were revived and carried out by his successors years after his death. He had a great respect for Indian traditions of domestic architecture. 'Infinite patience and indomitable courage', he wrote, 'have gone into these monuments of man's creative capacity . . . developed through centuries to meet the challenge of climate and available material.' The modern architect, he urged, ought to study these things with humility, so that his own work may be 'humanised and Indianised'.

Dann's work in architecture was a way of worship as well as a way of service; the two were 'one indivisible whole'. In addition to his official work he gave his time most generously to designing churches and other places of prayer, of which one of the most satisfying and beautiful is the chapel of the Women's Christian College at Madras, a place 'whose very bricks and mortar seem to have captured a spirit of worship'.[4] But there was no separation of the sacred and the secular; *all* Dann's buildings, whether church or hospital or univer-sity or ordinary dwelling house, expressed his standards of integrity: *simple* materials, *'truthfully'* displayed; nothing that was not *useful*, nothing that was not *strong*. They expressed too his imaginative use of tradition, and his love for the quality of *life* that was found in hand-made brick and hand-worked stone. This integrity, he believed, was the secret of beauty; he regarded ugliness as a sin against the divine loveliness of the world and an insult to the divine life within humanity.

Dann's buildings were 'the language of his soul', but the quality of his daily life spoke as surely to all kinds of people; household servants, petty clerks, troubled colleagues, impatient students all recognised his serenity and strength, and his readiness to listen and to care. Like Gravely, he belonged to an older generation than the young Friends who were so powerfully influenced by Gandhi in the 1930s, but coming to India in the midst of 'non-cooperation' he saw beneath the surface excitement to the meaning and power of the discipline of non-violence, and the wisdom of the principles of the good life on which Gandhi was trying to refashion Indian society.

Other Quakers of this older generation served India through 'official' channels, like the engineers, Guy Jackson and Theodore Burtt, who were concerned with India's basic need for the conservation of water.[5] The Quaker scientist, Joseph Hutchinson, spent what he felt to be 'the most fruitful years of his life' at Indore, where from 1933 to 1937 he worked on fundamental research in cotton with a team of Indian colleagues who quickly became personal friends. 'Understanding of the nature of the evolution of the cottons', he wrote, 'is the identification of a part of the pattern of life.' It led him to reflect on more complex patterns of life, and to ponder the need for an education which should 'span the range of social, economic and practical wisdom that goes into the practice of agriculture'. Hutchinson's thought was on a world scale and at a university level, but it had links with Gandhi's ideas for a village education which might enable 'social, economic and practical wisdom' to be applied to the local farms and the local village community, and with the pioneer work of Vinoba Bhave and Jayaprakash Narayan for the moral and political revolution without which such an education could not bear its full fruit.[6]

Another Quaker of Jack Hoyland's age, Percy Oddie Whitlock, also spent many years in education in India. Whitlock had been a pupil and then a teacher in Quaker schools before he went to Cambridge in 1907 as a scholar of St John's College. It seems likely that his interest in India was awakened at Cambridge, where Andrews's influence was at that time turning the thoughts of a good many young men to the possibilities of work in Indian colleges. In 1911, soon after he had taken his degree, Whitlock applied for a post in Nagpur, but for some reason was obliged to withdraw. In 1914 he applied again, both to the Maharajah's College, Mysore, and for the newly created post of Professor of English and in the Ravenshaw College, Cuttack, to which he was appointed. In addition to an outstanding academic and athletic record he brought with him from the various Quaker schools in which he had taught a double reputation – for good 'discipline' and for genial and happy relationships with his students.

Ravenshaw College was a government college, and Whitlock was a member of the Indian Educational Service. Towards the end of his Indian career, when the political events of 1932 had sparked off some heated controversy in Quaker journals, he intervened with the comment that 'it is possible to be a Government servant and fair-minded'.[7] His Indian students would have agreed; they remembered his fair-mindedness and his friendliness as well as his occasional rebukes. He was 'different' from most Englishmen of their experience; he broke through racial barriers, played cricket along with them in the college XI and took an interest in their doings outside class. When they picketed the college gates during the non-cooperation movement of 1921 he went down to watch, and presently called one of them to him. 'Is it true that Dr Rajendra Prasad is connected with this movement?' he asked. 'Yes, sir,' replied the student, 'he is one of Gandhi's closest followers.' 'He's a good man,' said Whitlock (who had met Prasad in Patna University committees). 'If he is in it, it deserves respect.' A few years later, when the news of Lala Lajpat Rai's death reached the college, some of the students impulsively walked out of their classes 'as a mark of respect'. Whitlock was irritated by the discourtesy shown to teachers, especially on the part of senior MA students. 'Why didn't you consult me?' he asked. 'I would have suspended classes, and you could have had a proper meeting in his memory.' But he bore them no grudge; soon afterwards, in dealing with another matter, he took pains to ensure fair treatment for the 'offenders'.

One year new buildings were constructed, and the students happily prepared for entry by swilling their new hostel rooms, Indian style, with several buckets of water. They discovered too late that no water outlet had been provided, and after laboriously mopping up the flood, one of them went to complain to the engineer in charge.

The engineer was annoyed and reported him to Whitlock for 'impertinence'. Whitlock received the boy rather sternly, but listened quietly to his explanation, dismissed him with a caution, and said no more. Some months later, when he had forgotten the incident, Whitlock called him to his home and introduced him to an Englishman present, the Chief Engineer of the Province. 'I'm told', said the engineer with a twinkle, 'that you want to know why there are no drainage channels from the hostel rooms.' All the engineering textbooks, he explained, had been written for *England*, where methods of floor-washing were different. 'Isn't it time you got some written for *India*?' asked Whitlock drily.

In class too he endeared himself by his informal, man-to-man style; he was not afraid to say 'I don't know, I'll have to think it over, we'll come back to it tomorrow'; he was not afraid to comment, in class, that if India could produce a leader of the quality of Garibaldi she would soon be free! An unusual style for a government college in the 1920s! It is said that it was Whitlock's personal popularity which kept the Cuttack college comparatively calm during the 1930 political agitation. Some students knew he was 'a Quaker', but that meant little; they judged him as a man.[8]

After 1947 there was obviously less scope for expatriates to serve India in such 'official' capacities, except in UNESCO or similar international organisations; Quakers like Ronald and Elsie Harris and H. Wright Baker were able to share their technical knowledge in this way; Ilfra Lovedee worked in a number of Indian cities for the WHO, and all of them enriched the Quaker fellowship. Sigrid and Diderich Lund, who had found that Gandhi's writings 'spoke to their condition' very strongly in the years preceding the Second World War, took him as their guide when their own country, Norway, was overrun by the Nazi armies, and played a leading part in the non-violent resistance to Nazi indoctrination which followed. Diderich visited India for the World Peace Meeting in 1949, and a few years later they both made their home for a time in Kerala, where he directed the Indo-Norwegian project of assistance to the fishing industry, and Sigrid shared in much Quaker and humanitarian service. The old Quaker link with the YMCA was continued through the long service of Richard and Edith Cooper in Madras, Bangalore and Delhi; in Madras and in Bangalore meetings for worship were held in their home. Gordon Muirhead, who with his wife Esther had first come to India in the Friends Service Unit in Calcutta, worked for many years for an Indian firm of solicitors, and they too lived in Bangalore, where they forged strong links between Quaker and Indian individuals and organisations, many of them inspired by Gandhi, whose ideals of community service were similar to theirs.

Benjamin and Emily Polk were attracted to India during the same period by personal contact with enthusiastic followers of Gandhi. Ben was an American architect, one who found that his professional life 'was guided at unexpected but crucial moments by his Quaker faith and friends'. He and Emily lived during their first year in rural Bihar, in the simplest Indian surroundings, while Ben experimented with rammed earth blocks in the hope that the students who were being introduced to Gandhi's ideas of education might learn to build their own schools and homes. The experiment failed, not because of faulty techniques but because the basic attitudes needed for social and economic co-operation had not yet been sufficiently mastered by some of those concerned.

The Polks then moved to Calcutta, where with Indian partners Ben built up an architectural business dealing with a great variety of work. His professional approach was like Reginald Dann's; he too felt called to 'interpret the old forms for this century', and he rejoiced in the joy they gave to the workmen who carried out his designs and the peasants who watched them build. Both in Calcutta and in Delhi, where the Polks also lived for a time, they were very much part of the Quaker fellowship, and Ben was active in the work-camps which Calcutta friends of Friends were organising among students in the villages. 'In the village I received, in the city I could give,' he commented.

Polk's own most distinctive architectural achievement is not in India, though it was worked on from the Calcutta office; it is a Buddhist centre in Rangoon, in preparation for which he immersed himself in the ancient Buddhist symbols and their spiritual meanings. India, however, possesses another monument of his Quaker concern. He designed the national memorial to the tragedy at Jallianwala Bagh, Amritsar, in 1919; his design, he felt, interpreted the desire for reconciliation already present in the Indian government leaders who commissioned it: Jawaharlal Nehru, Abul Kalam Azad, Rajkumari Amrit Kaur.

This book is not designed to describe or discuss the various Quaker projects which were undertaken in India during those and the following years, and through which the great majority of expatriate

Quakers found avenues of service: in Calcutta, where the FAU gave place to the Friends Service Unit, with its wide-ranging programmes, and then to the Friends Centre, and where Bill Cousins began to organise student conferences in co-operation with Donald Groom at Rasulia; in Delhi, and all the outreach of Delhi into areas of international co-operation and international tension; in Barpali, Orissa, where the American Friends Service Committee organised a ten-year project of rural development, which was followed by an urban development project in Baroda and by the VISA programme, based on Bangalore, which offered young Americans, Quakers and others, an opportunity to learn from India by service in an Indian organisation. Each of these deserves, and some have received, separate evaluation. They are listed here because it was largely through the friendships made in these projects, and in the city meetings for worship which have been mentioned, that the modern Quaker 'dialogue' with Indian spiritual aspirations was made possible.

From the very beginning of the Quaker enterprise in India there have been some Quakers who made friends with other spiritual seekers in a way which transcended their respective religious 'labels'. Elkanah Beard made such friends, both Hindu and Muslim; Charles Gayford and Pandit Govind Ram knew one another 'in that which is eternal', as early Quakers expressed it. If we had more personal records we might learn of similar friendships with Indian seekers enjoyed by Quakers like Wood in Bombay or Sturge in Hyderabad. Every modern Quaker centre, project or meeting for worship has attracted a number of people from various religious backgrounds who have felt at home in this way with the Quaker religious outlook. The great majority of these enjoy an intimate religious fellowship with Quakers which enriches both sides; they are satisfied with this, and do not feel any need to identify themselves more completely with Quakers as an organised religious body.

Among many such Indian friends of Friends two may be mentioned. Sudhir Ghosh (1917–67) met Quakers as a student in 1937, identified himself with the ideals of the India Conciliation Group first in Cambridge and later in Calcutta, and threw himself into the work of the Friends Ambulance Unit in Bengal. In some of the critical negotiations leading up to Indian independence he was Gandhi's trusted emissary. In the years after partition he and his wife Shanti played a key part in transforming Faridabad from a chaotic camp of despairing refugees into a forward-looking industrial township.

Arjan Dass, himself a young refugee from Lahore, began working with Ranjit Chetsingh in the Delhi Quaker Centre in 1947. He gave himself unstintingly to its service for nearly thirty years, until his health failed, a few months before his death in 1977. Neither of these men was ever a Quaker in name; each remained rooted in his own culture, and each worked with Quakers in a unity of spirit in which names and labels did not matter.

There are a few, however, who do wish to become Quakers. The first such seekers from outside the Hoshangabad area of whom we have any knowledge were Nalin Ganguly and G. L. Narasimhan. We do not know how Nalin Ganguly, a Bengali Brahmin, came to work with Hoyland at Hoshangabad; perhaps it was through Sushil Rudra of Delhi, who was himself Bengali, and who would certainly have been interested in Hoyland's plans for the school. Nalin's subsequent contributions to the Calcutta centre and to Santiniketan have already been mentioned. The other Indian Quaker to be closely associated with Joseph Taylor in the centre was G. L. Narasimhan, who was undoubtedly the creative thinker of the group during Nalin's absence in England between 1919 and 1921.

Narasimhan was a civil engineer of South-Indian Brahmin origin[9] who had been a member of the Brahmo Samaj and had married the daughter of a Calcutta Brahmo leader. His own permanent home was in Bombay, where he was friendly with the Karmarkar family who owned the *Guardian* press. Joseph Taylor met him in the course of his own visits to Bombay on *Guardian* business, and they became intimate friends. Narasimhan visited the Taylors at Hoshangabad and got to know other Quakers; it was probably at Hoshangabad in 1916 that he met Sadhu Sunder Singh, who deeply impressed him.[10] Through the Sadhu's Christian witness and the Taylors' friendship he was led to become a Quaker. We do not know whether his wife was still alive – there is no reference to her in the records – but he evidently kept his links with Calcutta.

Narisimhan insisted, rightly, that the Quaker message needed to be presented to India from an *Indian* point of view, not by books written out of an English background. Under his leadership the centre planned a series of Indian/Quaker tracts, somewhat as Baksh had done thirty years earlier. But, while Baksh wrote in Bengali, Narasimhan wrote in English for an all-India readership. His is the only tract known to have been published; it was a Quaker study of

Jesus, called *The World's Greatest Guru*. It is said to have begun by
quoting Gandhi: 'Fearlessness is the first requisite of spirituality',
and to have put forward a moving Indian interpretation of the
meaning of the Cross.[11] In the columns of the *Guardian* Narasimhan
tackled another question of importance to religious dialogue in
India: 'Can the Hebrew-Christian and Hindu-Buddhist streams of
religious thought unite?' In 1920–1 he shared in the discussions in
Hoshangabad which helped to shape the Mid-India Yearly Meeting; in 1922, even though he had not been baptised, he was chosen
President of the Bombay Indian Christian Association. He
accepted, hoping to be of service, 'and at the same time to liberalise
their thoughts on religious matters'. (He was deeply concerned,
among other things, to overcome sectarian divisions.) There are
people still living who remember his generous kindliness, and it was
said that 'there is a radiance about him and he imparts his peace to
all'.

Both Nalin and Narasimhan were accepted by the Mid-India
Friends, although their religious outlook was much closer to that of
Hoyland or of the Quakers in Madras. During the next few years,
however, the estrangement which was described in the last chapter
had begun. When the Chetsinghs decided to apply for membership
in 1932 they turned not to the Mid-India Yearly Meeting but to the
little Meeting for Worship in Lahore, where Ranjit was then working. As it was not constitutionally possible for this group to admit
them, they joined the Society through the foreign membership
committee of London Yearly Meeting, a body which had been set
up to deal with applicants from countries where no Quaker organisation existed.

In 1942 a Bombay businessman named J. K. Mehta, who had
been active both in the Indian National Congress and in the International Fellowship, through which he had met Quakers, made known
his desire to 'be a Quaker-Christian'. He was accepted by the
London committee on the recommendation of Friends in Bombay.
He felt strongly, however, that 'it should be unnecessary for those
resident in India to apply for membership to any body outside the
country'. There were many in India, he said, who found inspiration
in the teaching of Jesus and who would respond to the Quaker
concept of Christ as Inward Teacher. He urged that some body
should be set up in India itself to provide for their needs.

The result was that a representative committee was set up in India by which the London committee was guided in its decisions. But India is a large place, and responsibility for membership did not rest with a local group whose members could talk with applicants personally. This is the principle accepted by Quakers in most countries and the one which the Chetsinghs had expected to operate in Lahore. It is arguable that in spite of the obvious difficulties it would still be the best workable arrangement in India as elsewhere.

In fact the great majority of applications for membership from 'residents in India' were from people of Western origin who were attracted to Quakers either through their links with Gandhi or through experience of the spiritual help they had found in meetings for worship in Delhi, Calcutta or Madras. For all of them, the Quaker recognition of 'the Light of God' in the loving lives of men and women of many creeds or of none was a powerful factor in their desire to identify themselves with the Society. This was true also of Indian Christian applicants, who spoke of how fellowship with Hindus and others in Quaker meetings had enriched their faith.

It may therefore seem strange that differences of opinion should have arisen over the few Hindu applicants for Quaker membership. This happened first in 1938 when a Tamil Brahmin, K. Narayanaswami, who had encountered Quakers first in Europe and then met some of the Madras group in South India, asked to join the Society. His devotional life had been nurtured by the tradition of *bhakti*, particularly by the teaching of a nineteenth-century Tamil saint who had known the spiritual power of silence, and from time to time he expressed his devotion (like Prabhudayal Misra) in hymns of his own. Those Quakers who knew something of his spiritual struggle, the quality of his ministry, and the joy and peace which he found in Quaker fellowship, were eager to welcome him. Another Madras Friend who did not know him, however, hesitated because he was not 'a Christian'. In view of the lack of complete unity the matter was postponed; Narayanaswami was not admitted till several years later. He made his own position clear: 'I have been led to a personal devotion to Jesus which brought me great satisfaction. This has been specially helped forward by the witness and message of the Society of Friends. . . . The step I am taking should not separate me from my brothers and sisters in the Hindu faith, rather it will strengthen me to speak to their needs.'

This was the root of the difficulty, and it was not new; it was the century-old conflict between the belief that devotion to Christ could only be fully expressed by identification with a 'Christian' church or community and the belief that it could be lived out as fully and more fruitfully within the community of one's natural birth. This was the meaning of the debate between 'separation' and 'permeation' which had gone on in Benares and Hoshangabad in the 1870s and among Calcutta Quakers in the 1890s. We saw how they, along with Indian thinkers like Keshab and Govind Ram, believed in 'permeation', while Christian missionaries, including most of the Quaker missionaries, insisted that commitment to Christ must be shown by 'changing one's religion' and leaving the community of one's birth for a new social group.

The question has a special significance to India which is bound up with her political history and which makes the term 'Christian' a particularly ambiguous one. Right down to the 1920s, for ordinary people, it meant one who had separated himself from Indian traditions and was identified with the British outlook and British ways of life. The idea was encouraged by the tendency among Indian Christians in general to keep aloof from the national movement and to proclaim their 'loyalty' to the government. At the same time, problems of Indian polity were being discussed largely in terms of a kind of 'balance of power' between separate, mutually exclusive 'religious' communities – Hindu, Muslim, Sikh, Parsee, Christian, etc. In this context a Christian was simply someone who belonged to that community, usually by the accident of birth; it did not imply personal religious belief. Because of this it has been difficult for Indians to think of 'change of religion' or 'conversion' in terms of personal conviction or experience; it had a political connotation, it was a potential threat to 'the balance of power'.

Neither Narayanaswami nor Mehta thought of their religious experience of discipleship as leading to 'a change of religion'; they did not separate themselves from their original communities. Narayanaswami expressed his devotion in terms of *bhakti*; Mehta used the concepts of Hindu philosophy in describing his experience of the Inward Light and the authority of Jesus. At the time when they asked to join the Quaker fellowship most British Quakers felt no difficulty in accepting them as 'humble fellow learners in the school of Christ'.* In India, however, there were a few British and Indian Quakers who believed, as did the Bundelkhand group, that

---

* All Indian applicants for Quaker membership from outside the 'Christian' tradition have declared their desire to follow Jesus within a fellowship which does not require subscription to any 'creed' or demand separation from the community of one's birth.

'a change of religion' must be insisted on. The differing circumstances in Bombay and Madras resulted in delay for Narayanaswami and immediate acceptance for Mehta.

Early in 1946 Gurdial Mallik applied for membership under a very strong sense of inward guidance. He was then about fifty years old, a man of outstanding and saintly personality. Thirty years earlier, when a student in Bombay, he had belonged to the 'student Brotherhood' which had gathered around Chandavarkar, and Chandavarkar had introduced him to C. F. Andrews. Andrews inspired him with his own passionate love of Christ; it was in loyalty to Christ, as he told an American audience long afterwards,[12] that his religious pilgrimage began. Some years later he was sent a *Life* of George Fox to review for a magazine, and so learned of Quakers; later still, in Gandhi's ashram, at Santiniketan, and in Bombay, he met some of the Quakers themselves.

When Gurdial's application came before the committee in India one of the members commented that the step he was contemplating amounted to 'a change of religion'. The suggestion profoundly disturbed him; he regarded his experience as having been one of continuous spiritual growth, in which the past was absorbed and enriched, not rejected, and which was leading to enlarging horizons of love and loyalty. The months of uncertainty and of correspondence which followed must have been very painful for him, but early in October at a meeting for worship in Delhi something happened – some say it was Gurdial's own Spirit-inspired ministry – which overcame the obstacles and opened the way for his full and speedy acceptance into the Society. That these six months were indeed a time of deep emotional stress is shown by the extent to which Gurdial's own recollections of them became unconsciously distorted. When he looked back on them fifteen or sixteen years later the months seemed to him to have stretched into years, and a delay which was entirely due to the lack of full unity among Quakers in *India* was mistakenly attributed to the reluctance of London Yearly Meeting to admit 'a Hindu' – while in fact it had already done so in the person of J. K. Mehta. The upshot has been a certain amount of misunderstanding, and it seems desirable that the record should be set straight.[13] Gandhi soon heard rumours that Gurdial had 'become a Christian', and asked him about them. 'Yes and no,' replied Gurdial. 'Yes, I have expressed my love of Christ by becoming a Quaker; no, I have not left the community of my birth.'

For more than twenty years Gurdial gave himself generously, but not exclusively, to the Quaker fellowship in India; but he was never willingly absent from any who were in trouble or in need, and his Quaker experience only served to enlarge his confidence that the differences between the 'religions' need set no barriers to human brotherhood. The words 'a saintly personality' were not used of him lightly; he had the saint's transparent radiance, which enabled others to glimpse the Light by which he lived; he had the saint's unquenchable gaiety of spirit, and brought with him great waves of delighted laughter; he brought also the saint's challenge to human mediocrity: the willingly accepted discipline by which his life became a vehicle for the simplicity of truth. It was a life of consecrated vagabondage over the length and breadth of India, and its joy was poured, time and time again, into spontaneous song. He gave to many a new vision of what an Indian Quakerism might be.

In 1962 Gurdial visited the United States at the invitation of American Friends who had known him in India. One comment on his ministry there was that, meeting men and women of enormously varied religious background, 'he always carried their own religious awareness to a new dimension'. The Truth in him did not destroy, it fulfilled; it enriched and expanded the Truth that was already there in the other. This is a potential service which to many has seemed to be one to which Indian Quakerism may be specially called, in an area where 'the religions' have so often been used to destroy, divide and impoverish the human family.

The concern that Quakers might help followers of various religions to come together 'to practise the truth of God in the world' was the origin of what came to be known as the Fellowship of Friends of Truth. In January 1947 Horace Alexander was with Gandhi in Noakhali, East Bengal, where the latter was intent on healing the wounds of 'religious' strife. As they walked together through the fields Horace asked a question which had been in his mind for months: Could Quakers 'help to provide a meeting ground' where adherents of different religions might meet one another in 'a union of hearts'? He was not thinking, he said, of any kind of syncretism, but of a *fellowship*. Gandhi replied that of the groups he knew he thought Quakers the best qualified for such a task, 'but only on one condition: are they prepared to recognise that it is as natural for a Hindu to grow into a Friend as it is for a Christian to grow into one?' In reporting the conversation, Horace said that he was particularly impressed by the words 'grow into' – the emphasis on *growth*.

The Fellowship of Friends of Truth was founded 'to promote a common endeavour to realise the good life for all' by members of different religions who frankly accepted their differences. It never took root in India, though some of those who were associated with it there have enabled it to do useful work in England. Was this due to some ambiguity suggested by Gandhi's comment – was it to be not only a meeting-ground, but also a seed-bed for an 'Indian Quaker-ism'? Mutual encounters 'in Truth' have been part of the life of Quaker 'embassies' and centres from the beginning, and are likely to remain so. The centres *have* been a meeting-ground; at the height of communal strife in Calcutta, in the darkest days, Sikhs and Muslims and Hindus of good will turned to the Quaker centre as the only place where they could meet one another as human beings, and talk frankly and without rancour of the most sensitive issues which divided their communities. Every little Quaker meeting in an Indian city, short-lived and irregular as some of them have been, has had some experience of this ministry of reconciliation. But in it there has been no thought that the people who found meaning in the fellow-ship would themselves 'grow into Quakers'. On the contrary, people were attracted because Quakers accepted them as they were, were eager to learn from them, and believed that the encounter might help each to 'carry their own religious awareness to a new dimension'. 'Quakerism is one path,' commented a centre worker. 'There are others. Why expect them all to be one?'

Moreover, Quakers in India have protested against any tendency to grandiose and self-conscious talk about a 'Quaker mission' of bridge-building. Human relationships, they said, are ruined by ulterior motives. 'Only as each responds naturally to the other can anything of worth be passed between them.'[14] Nehru understood this when he commended Friends for doing their work 'without fuss'. So did Horace Alexander. An Englishman who met him on a railway journey in India, having discovered that he was neither a government servant, a businessman nor a missionary, asked in some bewilderment: 'But what do you *do*?' 'I was tempted to reply', reported Horace, 'that I enjoy myself – or even that I try to glorify God and enjoy Him for ever – but that would hardly have been decent!' A modern Indian Quaker of Hindu background recently testified that Quakers had taught him to '*enjoy* God'. It was this unselfconscious fullness of joyful life, from which love had cast out fear, which spoke so powerfully through Gurdial Mallik.

The second on-going concern is that Quakers in India should be enabled more fully and deeply to enjoy one another. Various attempts to bring them together have been described; none yet has been fully successful. The latest is the General Conference of Friends in India, started in 1959, which grew out of Ranjit Chetsingh's concern for 'scattered Friends', and which also provides machinery by which 'residents in India' may join the Society without reference to any outside body at all. Readers of the later chapters of this book must have been conscious, however, that many of the concerns which are commonly regarded as distinctively 'Quaker' lie outside the centre of interest of the Bundelkhand Friends, who are part of the 'world family' of Quakerism and of its Indian household. Quakers in India who subscribe to the 'universalist' outlook often comment on the enrichment which comes from making friends, in service and in worship, with people of other religions who differ from them in 'essential aspects of faith'. Most of us have yet to experience the enrichment which may follow from making friends with members of our own Quaker family who belong to 'some other colour of the heavenly rainbow'.[15] Yet Kenneth Boulding, the Quaker economist, has recently suggested that our great diversity is by no means a liability, and that one of the most important things which Quakers may have to offer to the world is the demonstration, in our relations with one another, of 'a unique spiritual flavour of love without much unity'.[16] As Boulding also suggests, this 'making friends' will compel a new faithfulness to the old Quaker testimony to veracity, a rejection of 'all that loves and makes a lie'.

There is also a need for Quakers to continue their dialogue not only with Gandhi's Truth but with his non-violence – that principle which has attracted so many Quakers (of *all* colours of the rainbow!) in this century. During recent years Vinoba Bhave has often declared that *ahimsa* (non-violence) must become 'gentler and yet more gentle' if it is to answer the need of our increasingly violent society. How does this relate to the Quaker principle that human beings must be *persuaded* – by an appeal to reason and conscience – and not coerced or threatened, however 'non-violent' the threat may be? An honest dialogue, backed by the kind of imaginative experiment which is also part of the Quaker tradition, might bear much fruit.

The last few paragraphs have slipped unconsciously into the first person. Any claim this book may have to attention derives from its being written by one who has been involved in the story, who became a Quaker through Madras encounters in the 1930s and has had the privilege of sharing in the Quaker involvement in India's aspirations to the good life, as well as in some of the weaknesses noted. One personal recollection may be in place. In 1957, along with Donald Groom, I listened to Vinoba Bhave speaking on Christmas Day in a South-Indian village. Here is part of what he said:

> The experience of the Spirit takes many forms; each one's experience is both like that of others, and different from theirs. And each one must express the experience, but when the expression is through language it is limited; human words cannot reveal experience completely. The great spirits speak little, they reveal through their lives.
>
> It is here that our difficulty lies – in differing apprehensions of experience and in differing uses of words. In our apprehension is both light and darkness; in our words there is truth and also error.

The apprehensions of Quaker life in India here set down must hold both light and darkness, and the interpretations contain both truth and error. But it is part of Quaker faith that 'the ocean of light and love' can overcome the darkness; it is the national watchword of India that 'Truth will prevail'.

Bibliography

Alexander, H. G., *Joseph Gundry Alexander* (1920)
    (Quaker concern about opium, Chapter VIII)
Baird, E. E., *Adventuring with God* (1932)
    (The Quaker mission in Bundelkhand)
Beck, Theodore, *Essays on Indian Topics* (1888)
Bell, J. Hyslop, *British Folks and British India Fifty Years Ago*
    (1892: The British India Society)
Braithwaite, W. C., *The Second Period of Quakerism* (1919)
Brayshaw, A. N., *The Faith and Practice of the Quakers* (1921)
Campos, J. J., *History of the Portuguese in Bengal* (1919)
    (Origins of the Indian Quakers, Chapter V)
Coffin, M. M., *Friends in Bundelkhand, 1896–1926* (1926)
Collet, S. D., *Rajah Rammohan Roy* (revised edition, 1931)
Dodwell, H. H. (ed.), *The Cambridge Shorter History of India* (1934)
Edwardes, M., *British India* (1967)
Friends Foreign Mission Association, official *Reports*
Isichei, E. M., *Nineteenth Century Quakers* (1970)
Kling, Blair B., *Partners in Empire* (1976) (For Chapter III)
Lelyveld, D., *Aligarh's First Generation* (1978) (For Chapter VIII)
Natarajan, K., *History of the Press in India* (1940)
Pumphrey, C., *Samuel Baker of Hoshangabad* (1900)
Russell, Elbert, *A History of Quakerism* (1942)
Shan Mahomed (ed.), *Writings of Sayyid Ahmed Khan* (1972)
Shore, F. J., *Notes on Indian Affairs* (1835–7)
Smith, G. C. Moore, *The Story of the Sheffield People's College* (1912)
Thompson and Garratt, *The Rise and Fulfilment of British Rule in India*
    (1934)
Tinker, H., *A New System of Slavery* (1974)
    (Indian indentured labour)
Wadia, R. A., *A Forgotten Friend of India* (1946)
    (Charles Forbes, 1773–1849)
Wedderburn, W., *Allan Octavian Hume* (1912)
Wenger, S., *The Lalbazaar Baptist Church: a Centenary History*
    (1909: origins of Indian Quakers, Chapter V)

Notes and References

CHAPTER 1

1 'The Cambridge Platonists, almost alone among seventeenth-century religious thinkers, transcended the rigid division between the human and the divine' (Edward Grubb, *The Historic and the Inward Christ*).
2 Francis Howgill, 1672, quoted in *Christian Faith and Practice in the experience of the Society of Friends* (184).
3 A contemporary pamphleteer (not a Quaker) included the merchants of the East India Company among these oppressors, for 'robbing the poor Indians of that which God has given them, and . . . decking our proud carcases and feeding our greedy guts with superfluous unnecessary curiosities' (*Tyranipocrit Discovered*, 1649, quoted by Christopher Hill in *The World turned upside down*).
4 They addressed everyone, including the king, by the singular pronoun 'thou'. In English the plural 'you' is now universally used, but the distinction is maintained in many languages, including those of India.
5 *Epistles,* no. 87.
6 ibid., no. 47.
7 'Wheresoever we find true beauty, love and goodness, there is God,' wrote Whichcote's friend John Smith.
8 *Swarthmore Collection*, vii, 111, quoted in Braithwaite, *The Second Period of Quakerism*, p 217.
9 Quoted by Badruddin Tyabji, *Indian Politics and Practice*. For the ambiguous meaning of the word 'Hindu', see Foreword.
10 The Meos were among the tribal communities who were converted to Islam by disciples of the saint Khwajah Mu'in al Din Chisti, but retained many of their 'Hindu' customs. The shrine of Khwajah in Ajmer was revered by Hindus and Muslims alike (S. Khuda Baksh, *Essays Indian and Islamic*).

   For information on the Sauds I am indebted to Professor Vahiduddin of Tughlaqabad, Delhi, who kindly summarised it for me from an Urdu *History of the Meos* by Abdus Shukoor.
11 Translations from Tukaram are based on those made by John S. Hoyland in his study of the saint.

CHAPTER II

1 *Siyar Mutakharin,* quoted by Reynolds, *White Sahibs in India.*
2 Letter from Edward Wheeler, 1782, quoted in *Records of the Chicheley Plowdens 1590–1913*, by W. F. Chicheley Plowden.
3 Isaac Watson, quoted in Brayshaw, op. cit., p. 179.
4 Advice of Meeting for Sufferings, the executive committee of London Yearly Meeting.
5 'I and my brother were dressed as little Quaker scarecrows. We were followed

and hooted after in the streets by troops of rude boys crying "Quack, quack, quack"!' William Sturge, born 1820, quoted in Brayshaw, op. cit., p. 197.

6 The word 'evangelical' means literally 'according to the gospel'. It usually connotes a type of Christian theology which stresses the authority of the Bible, the corruption of human nature, and the atoning sacrifice of Jesus Christ.

7 Travers Buxton, *William Wilberforce*, p. 41.

8 R. C. Sharman, *Memoir of William Allen, FRS*. William Allen (1770–1843) was a distinguished Quaker philanthropist and an intimate friend of Thomas Clarkson.

9 Quoted by John Kaye, *Christianity in India* (1859).

10 For example, in F. J. Shore, op. cit.

11 Charles Grant, *Observations on the state of society among the Asiatic subjects of Great Britain* (1797).

12 The phrase is H. H. Dodwell's (*India*, 1936).

13 *NO OPIUM!* by 'a minister and a layman', 1835. James Cropper (1773–1841), descended of an old Quaker family, founded the successful Liverpool Mercantile house Cropper, Benson & Co.

14 Evidence submitted to the East India Company in 1813, quoted in Max Müller, *What can India teach us?*

15 Letter to Mountstuart Elphinstone, 12 May 1818.

16 John Malcolm, *Political History*, vol. II, p 183.

17 Minute on the state of the country, 31 December 1824.

18 Memo on native education, 1824, quoted in Colebrooke's *Life of Elphinstone*.

19 Basil Willey, *Nineteenth Century Studies*.

CHAPTER III

1 The *Bengal* is referred to in G. M. Trevelyan's *Life of John Bright*, p. 23. A painting of her dated 1815 is in the possession of the Cropper family at Eller Green near Kendal. She appeared in Lloyd's Register of Shipping up till at least 1833. For 'Quaker guns', see Henry J. Cadbury, *Letters from the Quaker Past*, no. 15. The earliest example of the term given in the *N.E.D.* is from Washington Irving, 1809. The joint owners of the *Bengal*, Rathbone and Hodgson, were at that date a Quaker firm.

2 'If slavery and slave trade had been left to a competition with free labour, and we had neither made laws to abolish them nor given our money for their support, both would ere this have ceased to exist' (James Cropper, 1827).

3 For example, Joseph Haselden, son of William Haselden, shipbuilder, who died at Hugli near Calcutta on 13 November 1819.

4 The Quaker was Samuel Southall, in the city of London.

5 Quoted in H. H. Dodwell, *India* (1936).

6 Joseph Sturge (1793–1859) was James Cropper's son-in-law and had many philanthropic interests.

7 See *Slavery in India* (Parliamentary White Paper, 1834) and B. Hjejle, *Agricultural Bondage in South India* (1967).

8 F. J. Shore (op. cit.) suggested that such sales should be registered, and the children treated as apprentices with the right to claim their freedom when they came of age.

9 *Cooli* is a Tamil word meaning 'daily wages', and in English usage came to mean the person who received such wages. Indentured 'coolies' were often recruited from poor hilly areas.

10 The Forbes family, in the seventeenth century, were neighbours of the Barclays of Ury, and, like the Barclays, became Quakers and intermarried with them.

Not all the descendants of either family remained Quaker, and Charles Forbes himself was 'a son of the manse'.

11 The quotations are from F. J. Shore, op. cit.: J. Briggs, *The Land Tax of India* (1830); Bishop Heber, *Memoirs and Correspondence* (1830).

12 George Thompson (1804–78) was an associate of Joseph Hume and a fine orator in the cause of the slaves.

13 Jagannath Sankar Sheth was one of the founders of the Elphinstone College, Bombay, and a pioneer of education for girls.

14 At that time the tea market depended wholly on China. Commercial production of Indian tea was in its infancy.

15 See, for example, Charles Trevelyan's report on conditions in Dacca, 1840.

16 R. M. Grindlay, 1837, quoted in Daniel Thorner, *Investment in India*. Cf. I. Everett, *Observations on India*, 1853: 'India has never yet been regarded as part of the empire [i.e. as an *equal* partner]. It goes by the unhappy name of colony, a place . . . made expressly to be plundered.'

17 'Planters can't make it pay if they undertake the cultivation themselves. They therefore throw all the risk on the *ryot* and yet claim every right over him to *force* him to cultivate' (*The Calcutta Review*, 1860).

18 Blair B. Kling, op. cit. One of Dwarkanath's opium clippers, the *Ariel*, was among those forced to surrender her cargo in the action which provoked the opium war.

19 A contemporary account of the inauguration is reprinted in *Nineteenth Century Studies*, no. 4, 1973.

20 'We of the present generation can only hope to serve our country through our failures,' said G. K. Gokhale in 1911.

CHAPTER IV

1 Quoted by Rufus M. Jones, *Later Periods of Quakerism*, p. 644.

2 Letter to J. Bevan Braithwaite, October 1859.

3 J. S. Urquhart, quoted in Hyslop Bell, op. cit. A perceptive missionary, C. Bomwetsch, later commented that if the government before the Mutiny had paid attention to the Agra newspapers they would not have been so ignorant of public feeling (letter in CMS archives, 1861–2).

4 'The rising enthusiasm for conversion has already done much to alienate the people' (Report of a Company official, 1834, quoted in Dodwell, op. cit., p. 726).

5 See G. O. Trevelyan, *The India we knew*.

6 *The Hindu Pioneer,* Calcutta, 1835.

7 Article reproduced in *The Friend*, December 1848.

8 *The British Friend*, 1857, p. 289.

9 A decent British planter wrote that it was almost impossible to procure sober estate managers, and that it was considered 'unusual kindness' to refrain from thrashing the *ryots* (Scott-Moncrieff papers, Centre for South Asian Studies, Cambridge).

10 Sir Arthur Cotton, 'the greatest engineer that ever entered the public service in India', accused the government of allowing too hasty railway construction without adequate survey. There is much evidence that his indictment was justified.

11 The previous editor is said to have been dismissed for being 'too pro-British' during the Mutiny (Natarajan, op. cit.). The management of the paper was independent and included Indian shareholders from the beginning.

12 Wood left Scarborough before being finally accepted, and was admitted to membership later in Sheffield.

13 See G. C. Moore Smith, op. cit.

14 They were married by the English chaplain in Bombay in November 1865. At Martin's request kind Dr Thomas Hodgkin interceded on their behalf with Westminster Monthly Meeting, to which Martin's membership had been transferred, and which 'in the circumstances' did not penalise them for marrying 'before a priest'!

15 *The Times of India*, 1869. The reference may be to the Viceroy, Sir John Lawrence, who had been warned by *The Times* (London) of the dangers of 'too much haste to encourage the propagation of Christianity'.

16 Statement by N. G. Chandavarkar and his colleagues Lalmohan Ghosh and S. Ramaswamy Mudaliar, 1885.

CHAPTER V

1 The use of the French spelling may indicate a home in Chandannagar, the French settlement where many Luso-Indians took refuge during the fighting in 1756–7.

2 *The Life and Letters of Lord Macaulay* (ed. G. O. Trevelyan) contains a vivid account of Macaulay's preparations for study during his voyage to India in 1834.

3 M. M. Thomas, *The Acknowledged Christ of the Indian Renaissance*.

4 *The Precepts of Jesus, a Guide to Peace and Happiness* was published in 1818, and led to a prolonged controversy between Rammohan and leading missionaries.

5 An account of Jagat Chandra Ganguly was published in *Weldon's Weekly Journal* in 1862. This was the paper for which Martin Wood worked in London before going to India.

6 He got his information from W. H. Trant of the East India Company. Trant's letter (2 August 1819) describes them as rejecting idolatry, caste and the sanctity of Ganges water; he seems little aware of their Muslim connections. Cf. Chapter I.

7 Henry T. Hodgkin, *The Call of India* (1919).

8 *Christian Work*, as reported in *The Friend*, 1 February 1864.

9 At least one inquirer joined the Presbyterian Church, and lived to meet Quakers in Calcutta in 1920.

10 By Ormerod Greenwood in *Quaker Encounters*. Some information about some members of the group may be extracted from contemporary Calcutta Directories. In 1863 Mariano D'Ortez drew a salary of 60 rupees a month, a sum which even sixty years later represented a standard well above poverty.

CHAPTER VI

1 Correspondence in *The Friend*, 1858.

2 *Epistles*, p. 136.

3 The keyword is 'instruction', implying a 'one-way traffic' in which the instructor is presumed to have all the light; earlier Quakers expected to *evoke* the light already present in others.

4 Quoted in C. Pumphrey, op. cit., p. 11.

5 Letter to Russell Jeffrey, October 1864.

6 Letters in the archives of the Church Missionary Society, March 1867 and December 1868.

7   *The Friend*, 1 September 1868.
8   See obituary articles in *The American Friend*, 16 March 1905 and 9 September 1920.
9   G. Huddleston, *History of the East Indian Railway,* 1909.
10 This and subsequent quotations (unless otherwise identified) are from Elkanah Beard's letters from Benares and Jabalpur, in Friends House Library, London.
11 J. Routledge, *English Rule and Native Opinion 1870–74*. The author comments with appreciation on the unconventional life and work of the three Quakers.
12 Dr Lazarus had a high opinion of Rachel Metcalfe's ability, and tried to persuade her to take charge of a girls' school established in Benares by the Maharajah of Vizianagram.
13 Russell Jeffrey, *Appeal for Benares,* 1864.

CHAPTER VII

1   Daniel Corrie, after working in Benares and Calcutta, became the first bishop of the newly constituted Diocese of Madras.
2   References to him as Dr Mendes are correct, but he was not a medical man. He was the first native of India to obtain the Ll.D. degree, and Queen Victoria presented him with her portrait in commemoration of his achievement.
3   British troops were stationed at Hoshangabad during this period. During the Mutiny a Gond rising had been centred on Sohagpur, where there was also a military camp (S. B. Chaudhuri, *Civil Rebellion in the Indian Mutiny*).
4   There is an account of Bal Mukand's conversion in Henry Newman's *India Journal*, written some years later. I have offered an interpretation of the events which takes into account all the scattered references, and which I believe to be intrinsically probable. Dramatic suggestions of a near-riot do not seem to me to be consistent with the evidence. The *chutiya* is the lock of long hair left by Hindu custom on the crown of the head.
5   Such a hope was not unreasonable. Ramachandra, a distinguished teacher in the Delhi College, had become a Christian in the 1840s and was later readmitted to the fellowship of his *kayasth* caste; in the 1870s he was virtually head of the *biradiri* (Alter and Jai Singh, *The Church in Delhi*).
6   Rachel Metcalfe's share in this short-lived school is the origin of the story that she 'founded' the present Friends Girls School at Sohagpur. There is no historical continuity. A second girls' school was opened in 1884 and closed in 1887. Rachel did not found either of them.
7   Gayford's attitude seems to have been similar to that of Percy Dearmer, who maintained that Quakers should not be a sect, but an order witnessing within the church to their distinctive insights (*The Friend*, 1911, p. 239).
8   Her whole remaining property – less than £100 – was left in her will to her solicitor.
9   R. Burgess, *Report of the India Sunday School Union,* 1899–1900.
10 Their plight illustrates William Wedderburn's indictment: 'They sought justice and we gave them law.'

CHAPTER VIII

1   John Beaumont Pease had himself been active in the British India Society. In 1863 he went to Raniganj, an area which then produced 99% of India's coal, and whose major coal company had been founded by Dwarkanath Tagore. I have been unable to discover what Pease's business there was.

2 He abused opponents personally, and called the proceedings of the Bombay High Court 'a debauched imitation of law'.

3 There is no record of any contact with the Calcutta Quakers (see Chapter IX).

4 Wood's old Scarborough friends, the Rowntrees, had their premises seriously damaged by 'patriotic' rioters.

5 Ellis retired after about a year in office because of failing health.

6 Quoted from tributes by Sir George Birdwood and Sir William Wedderburn in *Concord* and *The Times of India*, 1907.

7 FitzJames Stephen, quoted by Michael Edwardes, op. cit., p. 311.

8 Rogay, a descendant of one of Charles Forbes's friends, started an 'English' school for Muslims in Bombay in 1882.

9 Sayyid Ahmed Khan had been Famine Relief Officer under Sir John Strachey at Moradabad in 1860 and had attempted to get famine orphans cared for by their own religious communities.

10 One of these was the future Sir Walter Raleigh, whose early published letters contain glimpses of Beck at Aligarh.

11 Quoted by Shan Mahomed in the introduction to his edition of Sayyid Ahmed Khan's writings.

12 For a description of the wedding see the minutes of Devonshire House Monthly Meeting, the London Quaker body to which the Becks belonged, 15 January 1891.

13 *Essays on Indian Topics* (Pioneer Press, Allahabad, 1888, p. 620).

14 Obituary article, 1911, in *The Pauliner*, the magazine of St Paul's School, Hammersmith, where Wood was educated. Another version appears in *The Indian Civil Service 1601–1930* by L. S. S. O'Malley.

15 The Chicheley Plowdens had a long and honourable connection with India. One of them was involved in the correspondence quoted in Chapter II, note 3. Another was one of the 'small and unpopular minority' of East India Company Proprietors who co-operated with John Bright.

16 The letters and papers from which the foregoing account of Arthur Lidbetter Wood is taken are in the possession of his daughter, Mrs Imogen Wilcox, to whom I am indebted for permission to make use of them.

CHAPTER IX

1 Letter to Sarah Allen, 16 August 1800, in Friends House Library.

2 In religious terms, self-interest meant saving one's own soul. 'Don't you want to save your soul?' asked Quaker evangelists of their fellow citizens in Hoshangabad, and were taken aback when they were answered sometimes with a resounding 'NO'!

3 'Human beings are born into fundamental kinship ties, and must learn in what sense and under what great limitations independence is possible' (Maurice, *Social Morality*).

4 F. D. Maurice, *1857: Five Sermons*.

5 Quoted in *Memoirs of J. Rendel Harris*, ed. Irene Pickard, 1978.

6 The young men who wrote had Bengali Brahmin names; there is no further reference to them in the records of the group.

7 A temporary marquee erected out of doors for large festive occasions.

8 A letter to *The Friend* from a Hindu in Dinapore, Bihar, was probably a result of Misra's travels. He also found a group of young Christians in Allahabad who showed much interest in Quaker teachings. Most of them were employed in the Government Press, and had probably been introduced to Quaker ideas by Gayford during his residence in Allahabad.

9   *Lectures in India* (1879), p. 485.
10 The incident is related, with slight variations in detail, in two books: *The Gospel of Sri Ramakrishna* by 'M', and *Ramakrishna the Great Master* by Swami Saradananda. I am grateful to Swami Yogeshananda of the Vivekananda Monastery, Fernville MI, USA, for pointing it out to me.
11 *The Indian Christian Herald,* 22 February 1883. Cf. the comment of the Indian Christian poet Madhusudan Dutt (died 1873): 'Christianity is a civilising agency, but my real feeling is Hindu.'
12 Early English Quakers were advised that 'reverent singing' in Meeting is 'not to be quenched or discouraged' unless it is done *in imitation* and not by leading of the Spirit.
13 Many of the facts in the lives of the leading Friends were recorded by Isaac Sharp after he had talked with them in 1892. Poornachandra also left a short biographical note, which is preserved in Friends House Library, London.
14 Samuel Baker referred briefly to the visit in a letter to the FFMA. He satisfied himself, he reported, that Misra was not using the Quaker name in order to ask for money, and apparently took no further interest except to allow him to stay two nights with 'a native evangelist'. The words quoted are Poornachandra's, but he must have obtained his information from Misra.
15 The manuscript volume, a large bound exercise book filled with a fine clear handwriting, is now in Friends House Library. It was probably among the Quaker materials which were handed over to Joseph Taylor in Calcutta in 1919 by the surviving members of Poornachandra's family, and after the Taylors had left Calcutta was preserved by the remaining Bengali Quaker Nalin Ganguly. Nalin died at the beginning of the Second World War, and in 1943 the volume was brought to Horace Alexander at the FAU headquarters by Nalin's brother, Alin Ganguly, as being something of possible interest to Friends.
16 'We do not come to a termination when we have found out one truth,' said Keshab to Newman during the conversation which Newman recorded in 1881. 'There is a deeper truth on beyond it.'
17 It is not surprising that Poornachandra did not find a publisher. His book's main fault is its great prolixity. A shorter statement to which he refers has not been found.

CHAPTER X

1   The condemnation of the idea of an Inward Light was provoked in part by extreme 'Hicksite' Quakers, who spoke in a way that seemed to belittle the value of the Gospel record.
2   Letters and articles in *The Friends Oriental News,* file in Swarthmore College Library, Swarthmore, Pa, USA.
3   Three of her grandchildren were to grow up to serve India well: a school principal, a doctor, a Christian scholar.
4   'No section of the British public now regards famine and disease as a visitation of Divine Providence' (Hyslop Bell, op. cit., 1892). John Stephenson Rowntree criticised Friends for concentrating only on relief rather than 'institute a searching inquiry into the causes of these recurrent famines.'
5   One of these was the construction of the embankment which carries the main road across the swampy ground between Rasulia and the Hoshangabad railway station. The work was organised from Rasulia with government sanction and supervision.
6   Quoted by Pumphrey, op. cit. Italics added.
7   S. Katherine Taylor's report of a conversation between herself and Gandhi in 1930 (script in Friends House Library).

8   Gokhale had published criticisms of the Government's handling of an outbreak of plague in 1896 which he later found to have been based on unreliable evidence. He therefore publicly apologised, and was abused as a 'traitor' by the extremist group which was responsible for the murder of the Plague Commissioner.

9   Rachel Metcalfe had protested against this practice when it first began.

10   From 1913 onwards a Quaker couple, Edward and Edith Annett, worked for the India Sunday School Union, but for many years before that there had been some close friendships between its staff and some of the Quaker missionaries.

11   The winnower is still being manufactured by independent workshops in Hoshangabad and used in the district.

12   In 1920 a young English Friend, Roderic Clark, who had been in prison during the war as a conscientious objector to military service, found that the idea of resisting a government order was something quite new to the Hoshangabad Friends, who had little or no knowledge of the Quaker peace testimony. 'In prison and not ashamed to tell it! *Could* it be right to disobey the Government?'

13   Chaitanya, disciple of Kabir, was a famous poet-devotee of Bengal (see Chapter I). His writings greatly influenced Tukaram.

14   Bernard Lucas, *Christ for India* (1911). Lucas is a Quaker name, and Bernard Lucas's books were widely read among Friends, but I have not been able to trace any connection with the Quaker Lucas family.

15   The risks were real. In 1936 Mary Chesley (Tara Behn), a young woman Quaker and graduate of the London School of Economics, who had been attracted to India by the ideas of Gandhi, undertook the pilgrimage with two Indian friends and died on the journey. Gandhi wrote movingly of her 'firmness of mind, purity, generosity and love of India' (letter to Jamnalal Bajaj, 21 May 1936).

16   *Nishkama karma*: action without desire (for results). Cf. the English prayer: 'to labour and not to ask for any reward, save that of knowing that we do Thy will'.

17   John Somervell Hoyland, *C. F. Andrews, Minister of Reconciliation*, p. 15.

18   Hoyland's notes of these discussions were published as *Christ and National Reconstruction* in 1918.

19   W. C. Braithwaite, *The Second Period of Quakerism*, p. 538, makes this point in discussing the educational challenge to the second generation of Quakers in Britain, quoting also from Rufus Jones.

20   K. T. Paul, reported by Gulielma Crosfield in *Workers at Home and Abroad*, May 1919.

CHAPTER XI

1   George Selleck, *Quakers in Boston*.

2   The phrase 'gentle discerning spirit' is used by Mildred Maw, who knew Nalin in Hoshangabad. His family in Calcutta at first refused to receive him and abused him for working with the hated British; later they were reconciled and he was able to live at home.

3   N. J. Bose was the son of the saintly and much-revered Mathuranath Bose, for whom Sushil Rudra had a great regard.

4   Paper extant in typescript; place of publication not traced.

5   Quotations from *The Modern Review*, Calcutta, 1922.

6   Hostile demonstrations against the British were not confined to Calcutta. In 1920 Jack Hoyland was 'hissed in open school assembly' when he took charge of the Hislop College High School at Nagpur, and several Hoshangabad missionaries had unpleasant experiences of racial hostility.

7 'It combined a deep spirituality, a sane outlook in religion and politics, and an undeviating standard of right and wrong. We long for its revival' (letter from J. Sinclair Stevenson, Ahmedabad, to Joseph Taylor in 1920).

8 See the *Guardian*, 27 November 1952 (Sudarisanam Memorial Number).

9 A. A. Paul had been General Secretary of the Student Christian Movement in India. He gave his whole life to the promotion of interracial and interreligious understanding, especially among young people.

10 Pestonji Ardeshir Wadia belonged to the same family as Bomanji Hormarji Wadia, Charles Forbes's friend (see Chapter III).

11 The YMCA co-operated closely with the Student Christian Movement in work for students.

12 Frank Squire (1878–1962) married Winifred Green in 1925; they lived in Calcutta till 1928 and then went back to Ireland, where he was remembered for his simple but sensitive ministry in worship. He must have helped Calcutta in the same way.

13 In these prayer meetings there were experiences of glossolalia ('speaking in tongues') and its interpretation, which were very impressive.

14 This booklet has not been traced. Joseph Taylor had undertaken, on Jack's behalf, to see it through the press in Calcutta; perhaps political disturbances prevented the completion of the project.

15 Khan Abdul Ghaffar Khan, quoted at a conference at Rasulia, 1941.

16 Thomas Kelly (died 1941) is remembered for his book *A Testament of Devotion*. The visit to India never took place.

17 I am indebted for this information to Ernest Ludlam's son and daughter, Martin and Pippa Ludlam, both of whom remember the incident clearly.

18 Gravely's letter, dated April 1928, is in the files of the American Friends Service Committee. The letter to which it was a reply has not been preserved, and there is no indication to whom he was writing.

19 John William Graham discussed Quaker attitudes to peace with Indian Friends in the Hoshangabad area, who at that time had little knowledge of this part of Quaker tradition.

20 The publication at this juncture of Katherine Mayo's book *Mother India* added to the resentment; Gandhi called it 'a drain-inspector's report' on social abuses, with no recognition of the work done by Indian reformers.

21 Agatha Harrison was part of the team but did not become a Quaker till 1940.

22 'You should work subordinate to some indigenous organisation,' said Tagore to an American visitor in Harry Timbres's presence. 'Only then will India be convinced that you are really working for her good without ulterior motives.'

23 Before her marriage Doris Hitchcock had taught in Madras, where she was one of the leaders of the International Fellowship and a friend of the Quakers.

24 *The Australian Friend,* June 1970.

CHAPTER XII

1 *The Friend*, 22 October 1920.

2 Material from personal memories and from the *Centenary Souvenir* of the Madras Museum.

3 Alice Barnes and her co-editor Mary Barr both made India their permanent home. Mary Barr has published a valuable little book about her personal contacts with Gandhi.

4 The phrase was used by Reginald Dann's wife, Freda, to whom I owe much of the material here used. See also obituary notices in *The Friend*, 1939.

5 Guy Jackson was one of the engineers responsible for the construction of the Mettur Dam on the Kaveri river, South India.

6 Quotations are from 'Reflections on a Research Career', a lecture given by Sir Joseph Hutchinson in Cambridge after his retirement.

7 *The Friend,* 24 June 1932.

8 Two of P.O. Whitlock's former students, Sri N. Kanungo of Cuttack and Sri A.N. Mukherjee of Calcutta, have been kind enough to furnish the personal reminiscences used in this account.

9 Narasimhan's brother-in-law is said to have become Dewan (prime minister) of Mysore State in 1922.

10 Sadhu Sunder Singh was the chief speaker at the Jubilee celebrations of the FFMA's work in India in 1916.

11 I have been unable to trace any copy of this tract. It is said to have been republished in full in *The Christian Patriot,* a nationalist periodical then being issued in Madras, but files of this have also not been traced.

12 At a talk at the Quaker Study Centre, Pendle Hill, Wallingford.

13 The date of the certificate of membership issued to Gurdial is 31 October 1946. Correspondence is filed in the archives of London Yearly Meeting.

14 Comment by Margaret Finch, teacher at the Friends Girls School, Sohagpur, from 1932.

15 The phrase is Horace Alexander's.

16 Kenneth E. Boulding is President of the American Association for the Advancement of Science. The article referred to was published in *Friends Journal*, Philadelphia, Pa, in October 1979.

AFTERWORDS

1 Frances Reynolds

One of the most attractive of the 'lapsed Quakers' who made some impact on India was Frances Reynolds, who lived in Madras from 1843 to 1855.

Our first glimpse of her is as a little girl of eight years old, standing desolate at her stricken father's side, and watching her mother's body lowered into the grave in the Croydon Friends' burial-ground. Elizabeth Fry, a 'near relative', was present, and the child remembered her words of comfort spoken at the funeral.

Nine years earlier Thomas Forbes Reynolds, her father, had scandalised his prosperous Quaker family by making a run-away marriage at Gretna Green. Formally he was cast out of the Society, but Croydon Friends' compassion rose above their rules, and although his children were not members the ties remained very close.

Thomas Reynolds, unlike his father, had no taste or head for business, and Frances grew up in poverty. But her mother's family had East India Company connections, and when she was twenty they arranged for her to be taken to India – for a penniless young woman in those days a passage to India was 'as good as a dowry'. At first Frances hesitated, but in the end she packed her sober Quaker clothes, and Madras was soon captivated by her quiet dignity, her beauty and her winning smile. Her father's younger friend, George Knox, now a company chaplain, was delighted to meet again the girl he had once met in England. A year later, in 1844, they were married, and for the next eleven years Madras was the better for the simple goodness of the chaplain's wife, whose evangelical Quaker faith permeated the whole of her life. It deeply influenced her son, who was to comment many years later on the tender loving-kindness he found 'in the borderland where Quakerism and evangelicalism met'[*].

To the end of her days Frances kept her Quaker simplicity of life, wearing no colours but those sanctioned by Quaker custom. She kept her loving charm, and captivated her four brilliant grandsons (E.V. Knox – 'Evoe' of *Punch* – and his brothers) as she had captivated Madras fifty years earlier.

---

[*] *Reminiscences of an Octogenarian* (1930) by Frances' son Edmund Knox, born in India in 1847. See also *The Knox Brothers* by 'Evoe'''s daughter.

2 Martin Wood and Philip Sturge

Since the main body of this book was completed it has been possible to consult the files of *The Bombay Review* (published 1878–81) in the archives of the Asiatic Society, Bombay, and to meet a number of men still living in Hyderabad who cherish the memory of Philip Henry Sturge and could throw light on the links between Aligarh and Hyderabad.

Martin Wood regarded *The Bombay Review* as his best work in Indian journalism. It has a more personal flavour than *The Times of India*, and Wood's special interests are prominent. Each weekly issue bore the caption: *We shall never know that we are Englishmen till we have lost India*; Wood saw the signs of that outcome in the Government espionage which 'undermines public confidence and breeds distrust', and the folly of Lord Lytton's suppression of the vernacular press, whose only result in his opinion was to replace good, cogent writing in Indian languages by poor writing in bad English! He welcomed any movement which tended to an all-India national outlook: the educational movement in Aligarh as well as the growing realisation that the sectional and provincial limitations of Indian political life must be overcome. But the subject which more than any other in these years aroused his concern, and to which *The Bombay Review* reverted again and again, was the neglect and destruction of India's forest wealth:

> The Famine Commission should inquire whether or not the plenty of the past has vanished with the forests, which are reservoirs without dams. . . . The old balance of nature, so carefully preserved by the Peshwas, has been wantonly abandoned by us.

A hundred years later, the warning is even more urgently needed.

The Bombay Review also gives vigorous expression to Wood's characteristically Quaker belief that moral standards must be applied to public life no less than to personal conduct. In this he warmly supported George Bowen's *Bombay Guardian*, while at the same time he condemned the narrow fanaticism of most street preaching – Christian, Hindu and Muslim alike.

Hyderabad had a pioneer school, the Madrasa-i-Aliya, founded by the great Salar Jung. In 1887 two Englishmen who were teaching in this school took steps to found the Nizam's College; Philip Sturge joined them in 1887–8 and in 1890 became Vice-Principal. Hyderabad at that time had a markedly all-India flavour; leading families from Delhi, Mysore, Oudh, etc., had migrated there when these formerly independent states came under British control, and it was natural that ties with Aligarh should be closer, and that – like Aligarh – the college was open to students of all creeds.

Philip Sturge was first and last a teacher rather than an administrator, though it was he who in 1914 moved the College to the pleasant site it still possesses. He is very warmly remembered by those who knew him, whether they were little boys in the street or students in the college, and the very jokes he made with the children are still recalled. One who was not only his student but in his last years was his junior colleague still treasures the personal testimonial Sturge wrote for him. Gentle, even-tempered, serious in manner (though a twinkling fun would suddenly break through), a brilliant historian and a lover of literature – and of cricket; one who never let the increasing deafness of later years sour his humanity: this is the word-portrait which remains. None of his students knew him as a Quaker; they loved him as a man, and honoured him for his whole-hearted dedication to his chosen path of service.

Index